M000190251

Love Notes

*Daily Wisdom
for the Soul*

Elizabeth B. Hill, MSW

Copyright © 2020 Elizabeth B. Hill

All rights reserved.

ISBN: 978-0-9991976-1-5

DEDICATION

for karla,
my soul sister through all the lifetimes

Daily Access To Love Notes For Free

To express gratitude to you, my dear reader, I am giving you all the goodness of my *Love Notes* book every day for free. Sign up below to have messages of love and wisdom delivered straight to your email inbox every day for a year.

Sign up for free here:

www.greenheartliving.com/year-of-love

ACKNOWLEDGEMENTS

First, I want to acknowledge my coaching clients. Your courage, compassion, enthusiasm, kind words, and wisdom guided me in writing these pages. We've had a lot to laugh about, cry about, and celebrate together. Thank you for your love and trust in me and in yourselves.

Darren and Barbara, you both kept me writing my Love Notes when I wanted to throw my hands up in the air. I don't believe this book would have been finished without you. I am deeply grateful.

Immense gratitude goes out to my life coach and dear friend, Kathleen Troy. I could not imagine going through the past few years without you. Your compassionate support kept me going through all the muck. I am eternally grateful.

I thank Hazel Bet, Karlie, Jeremy, and Audra for helping craft these pages.

Gratitude goes out to my parents, Papa Steve and Mother ELM Hill, for teaching me what love is all about.

I thank my Grandma and my Auntie Bert for being there for me through everything.

To my children, Raven and James, thank you for giving me the best adventure I could wish for and teaching me more about love each day.

Love and gratitude to my soul sister Karla, my sweetheart April, and Gabriella, the wise and hot.

I thank all the members of the Love Notes Launch Team. I am so grateful for your generosity, support, creativity, and love.

I express my gratitude to those that have danced with me in the immense mystery of love. What a wild adventure this life is.

WHY I WROTE THIS BOOK

I wrote this book to help people change their mind's backdrop from one of FEAR to one of LOVE.

I know that it is possible because I have done it myself.

Most of my youth and early adulthood I woke with panic and fear of the day that lay ahead.

At different times in my life, this panic and anxiety has taken different forms, including: sleepless nights, upset stomachs, inability to eat anything but lettuce and bacon-bits, drinking alcohol to deal with people, drinking alcohol out of the absurd belief that it would help me sleep, memorizing the fabric-make-up of the clothes in my drawers, hiding in basements, checking 100 times whether or not the front door was locked and the stove was off, cutting my skin with razors, cutting off most of my hair, pulling my hair out, sore throats, backaches, booking my schedule so full that I barely had time to breathe, shaking on escalators, and more than a few unmentionables.

I've been fired from jobs, disappointed friends, avoided conflict like a pro, taken jobs that required very little of me so that I could get through, failed classes because I was too nervous to show up for exams, and stayed in unhealthy relationships and living situations way too long because the alternative was terrifying. I've heard "I hate you, you are worthless, the world is ending, they're coming to get you, God will kill you" a million times in my own voice, from my own head.

Most people I know don't see any of this.

They see someone who has chaired meetings, earned her graduate degree, supervised interns, written and been awarded grants, raised two teenage children, taught yoga classes, and written and published books. I am their coach, their yoga teacher, their friend. They see someone who can usually smile, laugh appropriately, and be nice to people. Most people think of me as the calmest person they know. They go to me when the world is too much and they need a breath of fresh air.

I have been at the crossroads: do I choose to continue on my path of fear or do I choose to walk a path of love? I choose LOVE. And I have chosen it over and over again.

Choosing what we feed our minds on a daily basis is key to switching our overall mindset to that of LOVE.

This is the gift I offer my clients and loved ones.

This is the gift I offer to you.

Remember, Love > Fear.

"There is no fear in love, but perfect love casts out fear." –1 John 4:18 English Standard Version

How To Use This Book

There are many ways you can use this book. You can choose your own adventure.

- **Start where you are.** Turn to whatever date it is, at whatever time, and get some love flowing your way.

- **Begin the day.** First thing each morning, even before you get out of bed, grab this book and read the page of the day.

- **Journal.** Use the thought of the day to launch a journaling practice. Take a few minutes after reading to reflect on what the words mean to you and how you can use them in the day ahead.

- **Set an intention.** Each day the quote and reflection may spark an intention for the day. Choose a word or two, a phrase or an image to help carry you through the day ahead. You will be amazed by how setting a daily intention in the morning can have a lasting impact on your entire day.

- **Be random.** Flip through the pages and pick a random day.

- **Devour it.** Just sit down and read the whole thing. Why not get a year of goodness all at once?

- **Build it into your daily routine.** A strong morning routine includes: 1) Reading, 2) Writing, 3) Meditation, 4) Intention-setting.

  If routines elude you, write to me. I help people create routines that work for them like it's my job. Because it is. My job. That and magic.

dear reader,

these pages are a love note to you.

know so many are sending you love, those you know, those that you do not know yet, and those you may never meet.

love was written on your heart from birth and love carries you through each day, each moment, each laugh, each tear, and each breath.

you are light and came from light.

you are love and came from love.

i am so very glad you are here.

love & wisdom,

elizabeth

january

january 1

"The only person you are destined to become is the person you decide to be."
-Ralph Waldo Emerson

So often we start a new year
with a mighty long list of what we will DO
in the year to come.

How about we start this year by looking at
who we decide to BE?

love & being

january 2

"Take up one idea. Make that one idea your life - think of it, dream of it, live on that idea. Let the brain, muscles, nerves, every part of your body, be full of that idea, and just leave every other idea alone. This is the way to success."
-Swami Vivekananda

Oh, how I feel pulled in so many directions!

How to choose just one idea?

What lights you up? And is big enough to encompass all of you?

For me, it's LOVE.

That is my one idea. To make the world a more loving place. It's not one thing. It's a guiding idea that's big enough to live into. In this way, as we use our one idea to guide each moment, how could we not succeed?

What is your one idea?

love & success

january 3

"You've always had the power my dear, you just had to learn it for yourself."
—Glinda the Good Witch

Sometimes the ways we find our power are not very pretty.

There can be some treacherous, frightening, soul-searching, confusing happenings along that yellow brick road.

And what a beautiful discovery we make, if we pay attention.

We will have searched and discovered the power we have had all along.

It is not a gift we are granted.

It is a gift we had to begin with.

And it is a gift we are growing.

Brick by brick along the path.

love & power

january 4

"The definition of Sacred Success: pursuing your Soul's purpose for your own bliss and the benefit of others, while being richly rewarded."
-Barbara Stanny

What is your Bliss?

What will benefit others?

What does the world need?

Find the intersection of these three and your sacred success will follow.

love & purpose

january 5

"To be yourself in a world that is constantly trying to make you something else is the greatest accomplishment."
–Ralph Waldo Emerson

Thank you.

Thank you for being you.

Thank you for all the times you've stood your ground.

Thank you for all the times you've shone bright, even when others laughed or scratched their heads or worked to pull you towards something else.

The world needs you just as you are.

love & being

january 6

"A gut feeling is actually every cell in your body making a decision."
-Deepak Chopra

Today, listen to your body's wisdom.

Sit, get quiet, and ask your body what it needs.

Ask it what it's afraid of.

Ask it what it desires.

Ask it what it is hopeful for.

We tend to make decisions with our head.

Today, include the body's wisdom, too.

love & choices

january 7

"Whatever the present moment contains, accept it as if you had chosen it."
-Eckhart Tolle

Stop.

Breathe.

This is how it is right now.

You are as you are right now.

You feel how you feel right now.

It is neither good, nor bad.

It is as it is.

With acceptance comes power.

You get to direct your energy to create what you want. Rather than fighting what you don't. You are more powerful than you know.

love & receiving

january 8

"Gracious acceptance is an art - an art which most never bother to cultivate. We think that we have to learn how to give, but we forget about accepting things, which can be much harder than giving... Accepting another person's gift is allowing him to express his feelings for you."
-Alexander McCall Smith

By allowing the natural flow of energy exchange - giving and receiving in equal measure - we are showing compassion to ourselves and others in a tangible way.

To block the gifts and offerings of others, is a lack of compassion to others.

And to ourselves.

Let us practice the art of receiving, whether it be a physical gift, a smile, money earned or gifted, a compliment or a kind word.

love & being

january 9

"Remember always that you not only have the right to be an individual, you have an obligation to be one."
–Eleanor Roosevelt

The world needs you to be exactly YOU.

It's why you showed up here.

You have the right and the responsibility to be none other than yourself!

You, beautiful you.

love & responsibility

january 10

"Even if I knew that tomorrow the world would go to pieces, I would still plant my apple tree."
-Martin Luther

We will never know what will result from our actions.

There is no certainty.

We do not know what will become of our apple trees.

Or our work.

Or our children.

We know not what will become of our gifts, our projects, or any of our creations.

And how lovely to keep growing and keep planting. It's worth doing.

love & planting

january 11

"There is a force within that gives you life. Seek that."
–Rumi

What wakes you up, dear one?

What lights you up?

What makes you wonder?

What wraps you like a warm blanket?

Let's get some more of that up in here.

Put some of that in this day
- and all the days to come.

love & spirit

january 12

"When one door closes, another opens;
but we often look so long and so
regretfully upon the closed door
that we do not see the one that has
opened for us."
–Alexander Graham Bell

What door has just closed for you?

This time, let it close.

Let go of the door knob.

You don't need to be a kitty cat, sitting,
looking longingly at a closed door, waiting for
it to open back up.

You can turn away to notice the door that is
opening up freely before you.

Let it be easy.

love & ease

january 13

"Today is life- the only life you are sure of. Make the most of today. Get interested in something. Shake yourself awake. Develop a hobby. Let the winds of enthusiasm sweep through you. Live today with gusto."
–Dale Carnegie

The definition of gusto according to the Oxford English Dictionary is: "enjoyment or vigor in doing something, zest".

Gusto is like a partnership with spirit. It is the same breath of life that keeps us breathing and living. And we often don't even notice it.

As Dale Carnegie says, "TODAY is life".

Make the most of this day. Dance with life. Let yourself be swept up in the beauty of this day. It is all we are sure of.

love & gusto

january 14

*"Life gets better...when you make the
present moment your friend."*
-Rhonda Hendricks

The present moment holds a myriad of often
conflicting emotions in it. Anger, joy, pain,
curiosity, sadness, grief, uncertainty, certainty,
delight.

Wowzers.

That's a lot to be with.

AND, when we can be with all of it,
life gets better.

BONUS, when we can be with it and beFRIEND
all of it, life gets EVEN better.

How about we make life EVEN better?

love & friendship

january 15

"Abundance is not something we acquire.
It's something we tune into."
–Wayne Dyer

Living abundantly does not mean acquiring
more and more.

Living abundantly does not mean receiving
more and more.

Abundant living is something we can tune into.

As we are grateful for what we have,
more is available to us.

Often in mysterious ways.

love & abundance

january 16

*"To live is the rarest thing in the world.
Most people exist, that is all."*
–Oscar Wilde

Are you existing?

Or living?

This Wilde Life. This WILD LIFE.

Even breathing is a miracle.

Watching birds out the window.

Opening the pages of a book with wonder.

Cuddling under soft blankets that travelled around the globe to keep you comfy.

The eyes of a dog or cat so thrilled to see you.

To live fully is to see the joy, the wonder, and the magic in all of it.

love & living

january 17

"Sometimes your joy is the source of your smile, but sometimes your smile can be the source of your joy."
–Thich Nhat Hanh

Sometimes, smiles elude us.

Sometimes, even when we feel there is no joy to source a smile, we can find motivation to find a smile.

We can smile, as a whisper for connection.

A smile, that is a wish; a glimmer of what could be.

That smile can source joy.

love & wishes

january 18

"Learn to enjoy every minute of your life. Be happy now. Don't wait for something outside of yourself to make you happy in the future. Think how really precious is the time you have to spend, whether it's at work or with your family. Every minute should be enjoyed and savored."
–Earl Nightingale

I'll be happy when ... I find my love ... I move ... I leave this job ... I make more money ...

Chances are, if you got those things, you'd want something else.

Life is precious. There is no need to push off happiness to some imagined time.

Happiness NOW!

love & happiness

january 19

"Love and compassion are necessities, not luxuries. Without them humanity cannot survive."
-The 14th Dalai Lama Tenzin Gyatso

What if we could think of our compassionate acts as NECESSITIES, not extras.

What if we could lead our lives with that?

Compassion for ourselves?

Compassion for our neighbors?

Let's get our humanity surviving!

Shall we?

love & survival

january 20

*"Darkness cannot drive out darkness;
only light can do that. Hate cannot drive
out hate; only love can do that."*
-Martin Luther King, Jr.

When we feel overwhelmed by the needs of
the world and we feel the need to lash out
against the pain and the suffering and injustice
we see, let us be mindful of what we are
choosing.

Rather than fighting against, remember to
fight FOR. Remember to take a stand for love,
for creation, for justice, for kindness, for a
world where all have what they need and
opportunities for joy, work and caring for their
loved ones.

When we look out and all we see is a vast
darkness, grab a light. When facing hate, shine
love. Love for family, love for friends, love for
those we do not know yet, love for those we
know but do not yet understand.

love & more love

january 21

"Forgive yourself for not knowing better at the time. Forgive yourself for giving away your power. Forgive yourself for past behaviors. Forgive yourself for the survival patterns and traits you picked up while enduring trauma. Forgive yourself for being who you needed to be."
-Audrey Kitching

Honor yourself for getting through whatever you have needed to get through in whatever way you needed to do it.

Release yourself from the burden of how it was. And how you were.

All is forgiven.

With each forgiveness - of others and of ourselves - we gain more of your power back.

love & forgiveness

january 22

"Music seems to be the common denominator that brings us all together. Music cuts through all boundaries and goes right to the soul."
-Willie Nelson

We all crave connection.

Music has the power to cut through the things that divide us and get us re-connected.

With others.

And with ourselves.

It has the power to bring us home.

Today, amp up the music.

love & connection

january 23

"One channel is the Stress Channel and the other is the Peace Channel. We really do have a choice about what we listen to. The Peace Channel can only be heard when we are present in the moment, when we are in the now. To tune in to the Peace Channel, all we have to do is be, experience, notice, and naturally respond to what is arising in the moment."
–Gina Lake

When stuck in the muck, it's hard to see we have a choice whether or not we stay there.

But we do have a choice. We can get out of the muck. We have a remote. And we can change the channel from Stress to that of Peace.

First, find the remote.
Second, know how to use it (and make sure there are batteries!)
Third, change the channel.
Fourth, ENJOY THE PEACE.

love & peace

january 24

"When you do things from your Soul, you feel a river moving in you, a joy."
-Rumi

What is your Soul calling for?

What is your Soul longing for?

In the stillness, listen.

In the chaos, shake it up.

In the brokenness, open your heart.

Here you will hear what your Soul longs for.

Seek that.

This is how JOY moves.

love & joy

january 25

"Curiosity is one of the great secrets of happiness."
-Bryant H. McGill

Today, be curious.

How does it work?

What will it do?

Who will you meet?

Why are they here?

Why are YOU here?

Go easy.

Be playful.

love & curiosity

january 26

*"In order to heal we must first forgive...
And sometimes the person we must
forgive is ourselves."*
–Mila Bron

We are often way harder on ourselves than we
would be on someone else.

What can you forgive yourself for?

Forgiving others can be very healing for the
soul. Forgiving ourselves, for both our actions
and our inactions, is also part of healing.
Forgiveness, whether of others or ourselves,
is a sacred healing.

Give a little gift of the sacred to yourself today.

love & healing

january 27

"I thank you God for this most amazing day, for the leaping greenly spirits of trees, for the blue dream of sky and for everything which is natural, which is infinite, which is yes."
-e. e. cummings

YES!

All we need to do is look around to see the infinite majesty of each moment, each natural beautiful thing.

INCLUDING YOU.

You are part of this infinite, natural, amazing expanse of creation.

You are one of the YES's.

love & leaping

january 28

"We have more possibilities available in each moment than we realize."
–Thich Nhat Hanh

When you feel stuck or in a rut, stop and write ALL THE POSSIBILITIES of what you could do.

Even the ridiculous.

Even the very silly.

If you aren't laughing about the possibilities, you haven't thought of enough of them.

love & laughter

january 29

"Children see magic because they look for it."
-Christopher Moore

Children are ever curious.

They see the wonder.

They expect magic.

And so can you.

What magic will you find today?

It's there if you decide to look for it.

love & magic

january 30

"The creative process is a process of surrender, not control."
–Julia Cameron

Aaaah, this whole process of LIVING –
this is the greatest creative process of all.

What will you let go of today?

What will you release control of today?

Where will you surrender?

love & surrender

january 31

"If you want to see what you are thinking, look around."
-Landria Onkka

We are manifesting machines, whether we know it or not.

The thoughts we cultivate appear in our lives.

To change what's appearing, change what you are thinking.

It's not as magical as it seems.

Your thoughts appear in your mind uninvited, but you can choose which ones you entertain.

love & thinking

february

february 1

"Beauty begins the moment you decide to be yourself."
-Coco Chanel

You be you.

You are enough as you are.

You are beautiful.

love & beauty

february 2

"The soul is healed by being with children."
-Fyodor Dostoevsky

If you've become a stick in the mud, go find some children to teach you what's important.

If you think that you know for certain what's going on, go find some children and they'll tell you for certain what's going on.

If you are sad, children will get you laughing.

If you are lost, children will find you. Trust me.

One way or another, THEY WILL FIND YOU.

love & healing

february 3

"Limitless undying love which shines around me like a million suns it calls me on and on across the universe."
-John Lennon

You come from love.

You live in love.

You breathe in love.

You breathe out love.

The universe is shining a giant hug of love above you, around you, below you and through you.

Love shines bright.

love & radiance

february 4

*"Learning without action is like brewing
your favorite cup of coffee and not
actually drinking it."*
–Ajit Nawalkha

Ohh, that poor coffee!

Ohh, that poor you!

Give yourself the gift of taking action.

Action towards your dream.

Receive the fruits of your learning
and your labor.

Learning + Labor = CREATION

Which is another word for LOVE.

love & action

february 5

"Take a walk outside – it will serve you far more than pacing around in your mind."
–Rasheed Ogunlaru

Are your thoughts running wild?

When the mind won't stop, get the body moving.

Taking a walk outside – even for a few minutes – will shift things up and do wonders.

Feel the earth beneath the feet.

Breathe deep.

love & freedom

february 6

"We cannot change anything unless we accept it."
−Carl Jung

Is there something you are fighting?

Something that you want to get rid of?

Something that won't go away?

Anything you just can't shake?

Today, practice accepting it.

It doesn't mean we like it.

Accepting means we are acknowledging what is so right now.

Acceptance must come before it will change.

love & changes

february 7

"Your joy is your sorrow unmasked. And the self same well from which your laughter rises was often times filled with your tears. And how else can it be? The deeper that sorrow carves into your being, the more joy you can contain."
-Kahlil Gibran

When sorrow hits us, oh, how we beg to wish it away, to throw it outside, for it to leave us alone forever!

And yet, we could not have this sorrow without knowing the sweet joy connected to it.

Our capacity for one equals our capacity for the other.

So next time you are feeling deep, painful sorrow, trust that you will experience tremendous joy.

love, joy & sorrow

february 8

"I have to be alone very often. I'd be quite happy if I spent from Saturday night until Monday morning alone in my apartment. That's how I refuel."
-Audrey Hepburn

How do you refuel?

Being alone?

Time with friends?

Creating art?

Being around art?

Being outside?

Going to concerts?

Listening to music alone?

Your way of refueling may be unique to you.

Find your way and make sure you get to do it on the regular.

love & nourishment

february 9

"A book, too, can be a star, a living fire to lighten the darkness, leading out into the expanding universe."
–Madeleine L'Engle

If you find yourself in darkness, turn a few more pages.

Light is coming towards you.

All you need to do is reach forward.

Just a little bit.

love & expansion

february 10

"A *life spent making mistakes is not only more honorable, but more useful than a life spent doing nothing*."
-George Bernard Shaw

Don't beat yourself up for mistakes.

If you made a mistake, it means you tried.

It means you didn't let fear stop you.

It means you didn't let uncertainty stop you.

It means you cared enough to bring something new into the world.

There is an honor in that.

Keep going.

love & honor

february 11

"When I tried this morning, after an hour or so of unhappy thinking, to dip back into my meditation, I took a new idea with me: compassion. I asked my heart if it could please infuse my soul with a more generous perspective on my mind's workings. Instead of thinking that I was a failure, could I perhaps accept that I am only a human being- and a normal one, at that?"
-Elizabeth Gilbert

You are not a failure!!!

You are a human being!!!

And to be a human being with a creative, working mind that's jumping all over the place, this is totally NORMAL. Really.

Give yourself - your mind, your body, your heart, all of you - so much love.

love & humanity

february 12

"We are not here to curse the darkness, but to light the candle that can guide us through that darkness to a safe and sane future."
-John F. Kennedy

It is so easy to feel stuck in the muck and to curse the darkness.

And with that we will sink deeper and deeper into the muck until darkness is all there is.

So - next time the light's switched off - and the darkness is creeping in - grab a candle right quick.

Light that candle!

Light the way towards a safe and sane future.

And find others that are lighting candles too!

love & candlelight

february 13

"When we give cheerfully and accept gratefully, everyone is blessed."
-Maya Angelo

Today, when you are giving, give cheerfully.

When you are accepting, do so gratefully.

Most often, whether we are giving or accepting, we are also doing the other.

For it is impossible to give without receiving.

And it is impossible to receive without giving.

Either way, everyone wins.

love & blessings

february 14

"You yourself, as much as anybody in the entire universe, deserve your love and affection."
–Buddha

Listen to the Buddha!

He knew what was up!!!

Show yourself some love and affection.

You are worth it.

You deserve it.

Today and every day.

Swoon.

love & heart-shaped candies

february 15

"When it comes to love, compassion, and other feelings of the heart, I am rich."
-Muhammad Ali

Look towards your heart.

Whether you feel it or not, honey,
you are RICH!

Look for the riches you have right now.

love & riches

february 16

"To know even one life has breathed easier because you have lived. This is to have succeeded."
-Ralph Waldo Emerson

Success need not be elusive.

It all depends on what you consider success.

And to let people breathe easier, even just one, is the greatest success of all.

love & success

february 17

"Chaos may happen accidentally, but peace manifests by intention. Fear and anger may bubble up without warning, but courage and kindness grow through intention. Anything positive we want in our lives begins with intention."
-Lauren Rosenfeld & Dr. Melva Green

Do you feel disconnected from peace, courage, or kindness?

These gifts rarely fall in our lap.

But if we intend them, they show up
all over the place.

Today, set an intention to grow peace,
courage, and kindness. Set an intention to
embody peace, courage, and kindness.

And watch as you receive.

love & kindness

february 18

"You are very powerful, provided you know how powerful you are."
–Yogi Bhajan

You have the power, my dear!

If you feel powerless, look at the qualities that make you you.

Look at the gifts you have that are your unique light.

This is your power. It needn't look like anybody else's.

That's what makes you powerful.

Knowing your gifts.

And knowing they are power.

love & power

february 19

"The truth is, when you shine with all your brilliance and honor your value, you give permission to everyone around you to do the same."
-Margaret Lynch

You were put on this earth to SHINE and to SHINE BRIGHT. You don't need to hide your brilliance to make others feel comfortable.

When we set aside our music, our wisdom, and our ability to walk into rooms and captivate, we set aside ourselves.

It is not a kindness to hide our light.

The more we shine - the more we give others permission to do so, too.

Can you imagine how bright a world we'd live in if we were all shining our own individual lights?

Can you imagine?

love & brilliance

february 20

"It is never too late to turn on the light. Your ability to break an unhealthy habit or turn off an old tape doesn't depend on how long it has been running; a shift in perspective doesn't depend on how long you've held on to the old view.
When you flip the switch in that attic, it doesn't matter whether its been dark for ten minutes, ten years or ten decades. The light still illuminates the room and banishes the murkiness, letting you see the things you couldn't see before. It's never too late to take a moment to look."
-Sharon Salzberg

Don't be afraid! Flip that switch in the attic.

However long it's been since you peered through it, it is right on time.

This is the perfect time to see with new eyes.

This is the perfect time to begin again.

love & new beginnings

february 21

"I found I could say things with color and shapes that I couldn't say any other way – things I had no words for."
-Georgia O'Keeffe

There are many ways of speaking.

Some that need no words.

Art. Movement. Music. Play.

Find ways to speak today that require no words.

love & expression

february 22

"Now and then it's good to pause in our pursuit of happiness and just be happy."
-Guillaume Apollinaire

What if there was nothing to strive for?

What if there was nothing to make happen?

Let yourself be happy today.

That is all.

love & happiness

february 23

"However confused the scene of our life appears, however torn we may be who now do face that scene, it can be faced, and we can go on to be whole."
-Muriel Rukeyser

The strongest, most beautiful, loving people I have ever met have faced some maddening, confusing scenes of life.

You might not ever know it to look at them - or talk to them. They may make you laugh, they may be silly, they may sing you a song, or simply sit with you.

The wisest ones, the most compassionate ones, have been torn apart and made whole again. Often many times.

If you look out on the scene of life and feel overwhelmed with how it feels, know this and know this completely - you are whole. And this confusion - the feeling of being torn apart - is your strength, your gift. You can feel whole again. You can "put yourself back together".

love & wisdom

february 24

"Slow down and remember this:
Most things make no difference. Being
busy is a form of laziness - lazy thinking
and indiscriminate action. Being
overwhelmed is often as unproductive as
doing nothing and is far more
unpleasant. Being selective - doing less-
is the path of the productive. Focus on
the important few and ignore the rest."
-Timothy Ferriss

Hard truth today!

Look at your busy-ness.

How much of what you are up to makes a
difference?

Where can you intentionally slow down?

What can you pick as your "important few"
actions and give yourself permission
to let go of the rest?

love & slowing down

february 25

"People are like stained - glass windows. They sparkle and shine when the sun is out, but when the darkness sets in, their true beauty is revealed only if there is a light from within."
-Elisabeth Kubler-Ross

What kindles the light within?

Love.

Wonder.

Gratitude.

Play.

Creation.

Make space today to kindle that light.

love & beauty

february 26

"If the sight of the blue skies fills you with joy, if a blade of grass springing up in the fields has power to move you, if the simple things of nature have a message that you understand, rejoice, for your soul is alive."
–Eleonora Duse

Today, look up and see the sky: massive, vast, wondrous. Today, look down to see a blade of grass, a flower. In the countryside, suburbia, or the city, nature finds its way.

Today, look inward, and see the wonder that you are, each cell breathing, each movement a miracle. The simplest things of nature hold so much for us.

You, being nature after all, are cause for rejoicing. On days you don't feel it, it's okay. Stop, pause, breathe. Feel the breath move through you. Know that each cell breathes with you. Your breath is rejoicing through you.

love & wonder

february 27

"If only you could sense how important you are to the lives of those you meet; how important you can be to people you may never even dream of.
There is something of yourself that you leave at every meeting
with another person."
–Fred Rogers

Who will you meet with today?

What will you leave them with?

It's important.

You're kind of a big deal.

love & kindness

february 28

"Put your heart, mind, and soul into even your smallest acts. This is the secret of success."
-Swami Sivananda

Today, take one small act, and pour your heart, your mind, and your soul in.

And know that is enough.

love & success

february 29

"When you get into a tight place and everything goes against you, till it seems as though you could not hang on a minute longer, never give up then, for that is just the place and time that the tide will turn."
–Harriet Beecher Stowe

Dear one, hold on.

One more minute.

The universe has been curious how much you wanted this.

Are you giving up?

Pray not.

Hold on one more minute.

For the time has come.

love & the tides

march

march 1

"Forgive yourself for your faults and your mistakes and move on."
-Les Brown

Today, I'm forgiving myself for where I've gotten derailed.

I'm forgiving myself for all the balls I drop in the juggling-act of life.

I'm forgiving myself for over-committing.

I'm forgiving myself for the calls I did not return, the messages unsent, the meetings not attended, the mail unsent, the projects left undone.

What will you forgive yourself for?

love & forgiveness

march 2

"Everybody needs
beauty as well as bread,
places to play in and pray in,
where nature may heal and give strength
to body and soul."
–John Muir

Today, seek out a place of beauty.

A place to play and pray.

A place where nature may heal you.

A place where you can gain your strength.

Pick your place. If you can go there physically, do it.

If you can not get there physically,
go there in your mind.

Play. Pray. Heal. Grow.

love & beauty

march 3

"Man is most nearly himself when he achieves the seriousness of a child at play."
–Heraclitus

Kids take their play seriously.

They are passionate. They are determined.

Today, bring that passion and determination to your PLAY.

Your version of play may be singing, writing, telling stories, creating, or making things pretty.

Play lights us up.

It's not "foo-foo", it's not "extra".

It's important.

It brings us back to ourselves.

Our souls ache for it.

So, I guess you could say, it's kind of serious.

love & passion

march 4

"The spiritual path – is simply the journey of living our lives. Everyone is on a spiritual path; most people just don't know it."
-Marianne Williamson

Surprise!

To live a spiritual life, we don't have to do anything extra.

We don't have to go to a place.

Or be with certain people.

Or read certain books.

Weirdly, we are presented with everything we could possibly need for a wild spiritual adventure, right in the middle of life.

We just need to look around, and see, and know it.

love & spirit

march 5

"Nothing ever goes away until it teaches us what we need to know."
–Pema Chodron

Do the same things ... same situations ... same types of people... keep showing up in your life on repeat?

Usually people react by thinking they are unlucky, or something's wrong with them, or the world is dreadful, awful and broken, or people are wretched and evil, etc... As this keeps happening, it reinforces whatever idea they've decided is true.

Next time it - whatever *it* is - shows up, instead of having it mean something wrong about the other person - or you - or the entire universe - see if you can look for the lesson.

What is there to learn in this? What message lies for you beyond the initial gut reaction? Because, ooh, baby, it will show up on repeat until you figure it out.

love & understanding

march 6

"Never be afraid to fall apart because it is an opportunity to rebuild yourself the way you wish you had been all along."
-Rae Smith

So often we work so hard to KEEP IT TOGETHER.

Give yourself permission to fall apart - let go of control - let the pieces fall. Then step back - and get some perspective - think of what's truly important and the life you want to build.

From there, you can a build a foundation that is strong enough to support the beautiful life you've been wanting all along.

love & building

march 7

"I have just three things to teach: simplicity, patience, compassion. These three are your greatest treasures."
-Lao Tzu

What will you simplify?

Where will you show patience?

With whom will you show compassion?

Your treasures lie within.

love & riches

march 8

"Learning to love yourself is like learning to walk—essential, life-changing, and the only way to stand tall."
-Vironika Tugaleva

Often we think of loving as a thing we do or don't do - a thing we feel or don't feel.

But you can learn to love, including loving yourself, just as you learned to walk.

It might not be easy - or without a few falls along the way.

And it is ever as important.

love & learning

march 9

"The extraordinary life is waiting quietly beneath the skin of all that is ordinary."
–Mark Nepo

We miss so much in life
that is right in front of our eyes.

Today, stop to look at the ordinary
with new eyes.

Your home, the sounds outside, the trees, the pavement, the smile of a loved one, the eyes of a stranger.

This ordinary life...
there is absolutely nothing ordinary in it.

love & miracles

march 10

*"The most precious gift we can offer
others is our presence. When
mindfulness embraces those we love, they
will bloom like flowers."*
–Thich Nhat Hanh

Today, be with the people you are with.

Be present.

You don't need to bring flowers, money or
chocolates.

Be with them and be present.

As Thich Nhat Hanh says,
they will bloom like flowers.

I have a feeling you will too.

love & presence

march 11

"You get in life what you have the courage to ask for."
-Oprah Winfrey

What will you ask for?

Be courageous.

love & courage

march 12

"Grief can be the garden of compassion. If you keep your heart open through everything, your pain can become your greatest ally in your life's search for love and wisdom."
-Rumi

Keep your heart open.

When there is grief to feel, let yourself feel it.

When there is compassion to feel, let yourself feel it.

When there is pain to feel, let yourself feel it.

When there is excitement to feel, let yourself feel it.

This makes space for love and wisdom.

love & wisdom

march 13

"I am not what happened to me, I am what I choose to become."
–Carl Jung

No matter what has happened to you,
it is not who you are.

Who you become is up to you.

Who will you choose to be?

love & being

march 14

"I think of life as a good book.
The further you get into it,
the more it begins to make sense."
-Harold Kushner

Mmmm, this book of life.

If it doesn't make sense yet, stick with it.

Just a few more pages...

love & mystery

march 15

"Twenty years from now you will be more disappointed by the things that you didn't do than by the ones you did do."
-Mark Twain

What is it your heart longs to do?

Live without regret.

love & courage

march 16

"In order to be happy oneself it is necessary to make at least one other person happy."
-Theodor Reik

Who will you make happy today?

love & happiness

march 17

"God's dream is that you and I and all of us will realize that we are family, that we are made for togetherness, for goodness, and for compassion."
-Desmund Tutu

Hello, family.

We were made for goodness.

We were made for compassion.

We were made to be together.

love & dreaming

march 18

"When I dare to be powerful – to use my strength in the service of my vision, then it becomes less and less important whether I am afraid."
–Audre Lorde

Fear can stop us from moving forward and taking action.

When we feel shaken, look at your reason for moving forward.

What is your vision?

What is your purpose?

When we are clearly focused on our vision and bring all our strength to meet it, fear no longer matters.

The vision matters.

Our strength will rise to meet our fear.

love & vision

march 19

"Love and peace of mind do protect us. They allow us to overcome the problems that life hands us. They teach us to survive... to live now... to have the courage to confront each day."
-Bernie Siegel

Sometimes life hands us problems that we can do something about - and sometimes life hands us problems we can't do anything about - and sometimes it's a mystery which is which.

Whether the problems we're handed are "fixable", one thing we can ALWAYS do is to cultivate love and peace of mind.

Love and peace of mind hold us and give us the courage for each day.

love & courage

march 20

"I love you just the way you are."
-Fred Rogers

Me too.

love & being

march 21

"Infuse your life with action. Don't wait for it to happen. Make it happen. Make your own future. Make your own hope. Make your own love. And whatever your beliefs, honor your creator, not by passively waiting for grace to come down from upon high, but by doing what you can to make grace happen... yourself, right now, right down here on Earth."
-Bradley Whitford

What action can you take today to create the life you want? It could be a big, bold leap. It could be a small, easy step.

The size of the step is not important.

What's important is that the step is in the direction of the future you desire. The step could be in work, in love, in home, in connection. A step or a leap, the universe is watching.

Grace flows. Grace follows.

love & action

march 22

"Love begins by taking care of the closest ones – the ones at home."
–Mother Teresa

Today, focus on the ones at home.

Most especially, you.

How will you show your loved ones some care today?

How will you show yourself some care today?

love & care

march 23

"If you want to be happy, be."
-Leo Tolstoy

Drop the sense that you need to do and achieve and accomplish in order to be happy.

You don't need to do anything extra.

You don't need to impress or be flashy or check off the lists to be happy.

Close your eyes, sit, breathe.

You are enough.

I am happy you are here.

love & being

march 24

"Nature is not a place to visit. It is home."
-Gary Snyder

Nurture yourself today.

Be in nature.

It will not fail you.

And be with *your* nature - your own unique spark that makes you you.

It won't fail you either.

love & nature

march 25

"In the sweetness of friendship let there be laughter, and sharing of pleasures. For in the dew of little things the heart finds its morning and is refreshed."
-Khalil Gibran

Find refreshment in the little things.

Laughter.

Simple pleasures.

Sweet friendship.

love & laughter

march 26

"Remember your dreams and fight for them. You must know what you want from life. There is just one thing that makes your dream become impossible: the fear of failure."
-Paulo Coelho

Is failure embarrassing?

Is failure for fools?

Is failure for losers?

Or is failure the only way to learn?

To succeed?

To be the best?

To hone your craft?

The way to win?

Whatever you decide it means, will be what it means for you.

love & possibility

march 27

"In the name of God, stop a moment, cease your work, look around you."
-Leo Tolstoy

Set down your work.

Look up.

Look around.

Who are these people that surround you?

What are these things that surround you?

What is this air that you breathe?

What is present,
that might have gone unnoticed?

love & looking

march 28

"Do not let the behavior of others destroy your inner peace."
-The 14th Dalai Lama Tenzin Gyatso

We can't change the wack-a-doo things people do, but we can change how we respond to them.

We can choose our thoughts.

We can choose our actions.

And our thoughts and our actions have a very large influence on our feelings.

In this way, we can choose peace.

Over and over again.

love & peace

march 29

"I always knew I was a star. And now, the rest of the world seems to agree with me."
–Freddie Mercury

You're a star!

Discover yourself first - and at some point the rest of the world will figure it out.

love & stardom

march 30

"Keep only those things that speak to your heart. Then take the plunge and discard all the rest. By doing this, you can reset your life and embark on a new lifestyle."
-Marie Kondo

Take some time today to sit with your things - to see what speaks to your heart - and what does not.

Give yourself permission to clear and simplify.

love & freedom

march 31

"Rest until you feel like playing, then play until you feel like resting, period. Never do anything else."
-Martha Beck

To be your very best,

You must learn to play and rest.

Your assignment for today...

Is to rest, then to play.

love & play

april

april 1

"The most difficult thing is the decision to act, the rest is merely tenacity. The fears are paper tigers. You can do anything you decide to do. You can act to change and control your life; and the procedure, the process is its own reward."
-Amelia Earhart

Fear can keep us stuck in the muck for years.

Today, pick one thing you are stuck in the muck about...

And make a decision.

love & decisions

april 2

"I've been searching for ways to heal myself, and I've found that kindness is the best way."
-Lady Gaga

Spread a bit of kindness today.

A little kindness for others.

A little kindness for you.

Share the love.

And feel it coming back.

love & kindness

april 3

"If you want to conquer the anxiety of life, live in the moment, live in the breath."
–Amit Ray

Anxiety and stress can pull big tricks on us. They can pull us out of our bodies, while simultaneously sending our bodies into a total panic. Our physical bodies feel it and our brain tries to run away from it at the same time.

To get out of the anxiety and this stress-response, we can ground ourselves, coming back to the body and the present moment. The most reliable way to do that is to come back to the breath.

To feel the breath in as we are breathing in.

To feel the breath out as we are breathing out.

Again and again.

Until we come home.

love & breathing

april 4

"That love is all there is,
is all we know of love."
-Emily Dickinson

Today, let love be all there is.

And let that be enough.

love & all there is

april 5

"Focus on you – your soul, spirit, blessing people with who you are, and following your heart's passions."
–Ally Brooke

You, being you, are a blessing.

Today, follow your heart's passions.

Express your spirit.

Feel into your soul.

You be you.

You bless people by being who you are.

love & blessings

april 6

*"Take rest, the field that has rested
yields a beautiful crop."*
-Ovid

Create space in these days and nights ahead.

Space for sleep.

Space for ease.

Space for a bit of spacing out.

To receive a beautiful crop, we must do more
than sow seeds.

We must also allow space for rest.

love & slumber

april 7

"No person, no place, and no thing has any power over us, for 'we' are the only thinkers in our mind. When we create peace and harmony and balance in our minds, we will find it in our lives."
-Louise L. Hay

Don't let anyone take your power from you.

You have the power in any moment to create peace, to create harmony, to create balance.

And no one, no thing, no place, can take that away from you.

You've had the power all along, my dear.

love & power

april 8

"When life gives you Monday, dip it in glitter and sparkle all day."
-Ella Woodward

We have a lot of power in life - more than we usually realize - to switch things up and change the direction and the day-to-day experience of our lives.

However, even when we do that, sometimes we have to face things we'd rather not face. This could be a Monday morning at a job we aren't thrilled about - or phone calls we are dreading - or doing our taxes - or anything that we'd rather not do but feels important or necessary.

Regardless of the details, we can choose how we are living it. We can live it with annoyance or we can live it with a laugh. We can live it with dread or we can face it with sparkle.

We can use any situation to find connection with another or with ourselves.

love & glitter

april 9

"When you feel your life is blessed, the blessings multiply.
That is a law of nature."
-Oprah Winfrey

Look for the blessings in your life. Big and small. Write them down and at the end of the day, add some more.

When you look for and expect to see blessings, you will experience more and more each day.

This you can trust and rely upon,
same as good ol' gravity.

It is a law of nature.

love & blessings

april 10

"This self-love is the instrument of our preservation; it resembles the provision for the perpetuity of mankind:
it is necessary."
-Voltaire

Self-love and self-care are often equated with bubble baths and manicures and chocolate.

I am a big fan of all three.

But the greatest act of self-love is to create a life that we don't need to escape from.

What could you do today to add some deep self-care and self-love to your life?

Maybe it's saying no to something or someone, or letting an unhealthy person leave your life, or setting aside time that is
yours and yours alone.

I invite you to view these changes not as luxuries, but as necessities.

love & preservation

april 11

"*Stillness and empty space give rise to painful feelings. Rather than experience the pain, busyness becomes your drug of choice.*"
-Barbara Stanny

"How are you?"

"So busy."

How do you react to a moment alone in quiet?

Busyness numbs just as drugs, alcohol, or TV.

Busyness may make you look good.

Notice if your busyness has become an escape.

Cultivate stillness. Cultivate quiet.

Magic arises when we learn to be with it all.

love & stillness

april 12

"We are all one light on this one Earth, and loving humanity makes all the difference."
-Michelle Cruz-Rosado

Find one thing to do today to show your love for humanity.

As simple as a smile, sharing a laugh or a story, sitting and listening.

Look for your shared light.

love & light

april 13

"You alone are enough. You have nothing to prove to anyone."
-Maya Angelou

Dear one, you are more than enough.

You can enjoy who you are.

We are blessed to have you here.

love & joy

april 14

"*One thing: you have to walk, and create the way by your walking; you will not find a ready-made path... You will have to create the path by walking yourself; the path is not ready-made, lying there and waiting for you. It is just like the sky: the birds fly, but they don't leave any footprints. You cannot follow them; there are no footprints left behind.*"
-Osho

The path ahead may not be clear.

Trust that you will create it.

One step at a time.

You will find your way.

love & walking

april 15

"Change your life today. Don't gamble on the future, act now, without delay."
-Simone de Beauvoir

We don't know what the future will hold.

If there are things you dream of or want in your life, don't wait for a future time.

Take one little action towards your dreams today.

love & action

april 16

"Only I can change my life.
No one can do it for me."
–Carol Burnett

If you are stressed out, maxed out,
carrying the world on your shoulders,
I have some rough news.

No one is going to rescue you.

((((Eeeek!!!!))))

You may be waiting for someone to notice
your struggle. You may be waiting for
someone to step in to save you. You may have
even been TOLD by someone that they'd save
you. You may very well be the kind of person
who would do this for others.

You deserve not to wait any longer.

Drop the world for a moment. Decide which
things to pick back up. Only you can change
your life. And that's a good thing. Since only
you know exactly what you'd like to change.

love & changes

april 17

"When I'm tired, I rest. I say,
'I can't be a superwoman today'."
-Jada Pinkett Smith

If you are tired, consider this your message to rest.

Put down your cape.

Even superpeople get a break today.

love & rest

april 18

"When you plant a seed of love,
it is you that blossoms."
-Ma Jaya Sati Bhagavati

What seeds of love will you plant today?

They will grow easy.

Start with you.

love & growth

april 19

"The key that unlocks energy is desire. It's also the key to a long and interesting life. If we expect to create any drive, any real force within ourselves, we have to get excited."
-Earl Nightingale

What do you desire?

What excites you?

What drives you?

Today, let that flame grow.

Or, if it's dimmed, take some time to rekindle that spark.

love & desire

april 20

"Each of us has a unique part to play in the healing of the world."
-Marianne Williamson

Healing.

Sometimes it's the earth we walk on.

Sometimes it's the thoughts we think.

Sometimes it's the family pattern
we switch up.

Sometimes it's the heart that needs mending.

Sometimes it's the bone that needs mending.

Sometimes it's you.

Sometimes it's me.

Always, it's we.

Wherever, however, we are focused on
healing, we heal a part of the world.

And each of us plays a unique part in that.

love & healing

april 21

*"I work very hard, and I play very hard.
I'm grateful for life. And I live it –
I believe life loves the liver of it. I live it."*
–Maya Angelou

How will you love life today?

You could express your love in DOING.

You could express your love by BEING.

It may be a little of both.

love & living

april 22

"Rest when you're weary. Refresh and renew yourself, your body, your mind, your spirit. Then get back to work."
-Ralph Marston

Making the choice to rest does not need to be hard.

Yet, often we fight it.

If you are tired, it's okay to rest.

Whether it's your brain, your body, or your spirit...

All need rest sometimes.

Rest when you are tired.

Let it be an easy choice.

You will stand up renewed.

love & rest

april 23

"Breathing In, I calm my body.
Breathing out, I smile.
Dwelling in this present moment,
I know this is a wonderful moment."
−Thich Nhat Hanh

When we connect with each present moment, no matter what it brings with it, we can access wonder, calm and peace.

Try this 2-breath practice:

Breathing in, calming the body.

Breathing out, smiling.

Breathing in, dwelling in the present moment.

Breathing out, knowing this is a wonder-full moment.

Wonder - FULL.

Each moment is full of wonder,
no matter what it brings with it.

love & wonder

april 24

"The best way to not feel hopeless is to get up and do something. Don't wait for good things to happen to you. If you go out and make some good things happen, you will fill the world with hope, you will fill yourself with hope."
–Barack Obama

What good can you get out and make happen today?

It needn't be massive.

Even small actions bring big good.

love & hope

april 25

"This is the real secret of life – to be completely engaged with what you are doing in the here and now. And instead of calling it work, realize it is play."
–Alan Watts

Today, in all your work, find the play.

Laughter.

Discovery.

Creation.

Delight.

love & play

april 26

"Love and work are to people what water and sunshine are to plants."
–Jonathan Haidt

Get your water – share some love today.

Get your sunshine – work at something you enjoy today.

And feel yourself, grow, grow, GROW!

love & work

april 27

"*Nature does not hurry, yet everything is accomplished.*"
-Lao Tzu

Today, go easy.

No need to rush.

Trust that all that needs to be accomplished, will be accomplished.

It is the nature of things.

love & trust

april 28

"It takes courage to show up and become who you really are."
-e.e. cummings

Life takes courage.

It takes courage to show up, some days.

It takes courage to be you, some days.

It takes courage to allow yourself to grow into who you really are.

And the world needs that.

The world needs you, you courageous being.

love & becoming

april 29

"The beginning of love is to let those we love be perfectly themselves, and not to twist them to fit our own image. Otherwise we love only the reflection of ourselves we find in them."
-Thomas Merton

Today, let those you love, be perfectly themselves.

Love them for who they are, not who you are.

Love them for who they are,
not who you see they could be.

If you feel your love doing carnival tricks...

If you are trying to twist them up into you...

Step back.

You can, perhaps, start loving again
from the beginning.

You can always begin again.

love & beginning

april 30

"Joy is prayer; Joy is strength; Joy is love."
-Mother Teresa

Find your joy as a prayer.

Find your joy as a source of strength.

Find your joy as an expression of love;
love for you and yours.

En-Joy this day.

love & joy

may

may 1

"You are enough. You were born being enough. Nothing you say or do will ever add to or subtract from who you are."
–Jenny Layton

You needn't do anything extra,

Or do anything to impress.

You needn't flash your certificates,

Or dress to impress.

You being you,

Reminds me to be me.

And nothing is more extra,

Than US being WE.

love & poetry

may 2

"Do not wait; the time will never be 'just right.' Start where you stand, and work with whatever tools you may have at your command, and better tools will be found as you go along."
-George Herbert

Start where you stand.

Take one step forward.

Even if you do not know the how.

Or you don't feel ready.

Or your ducks are all over the place.

They'll never get all in a row.

Start now, where you stand.

love & trust

may 3

"Don't let the behavior of others destroy your inner peace."
−The 14th Dalai Lama Tenzin Gyatso

We can't change what people say or do, but we can change how we respond - externally and internally.

Accept what is so right now (whether we like it or not, judge it or not).

Drop the fight against reality (whether we like it or not, judge it or not).

If you can do something about it,
do something about it.

If you can't do something about it,
breathe with it, be with it.

Let what you can do be enough.

You deserve peace.

love & acceptance

may 4

"Today I choose life. Every morning when I wake up I can choose joy, happiness, negativity, pain... To feel the freedom that comes from being able to continue to make mistakes and choices – today I choose to feel life, not to deny my humanity but embrace it."
-Kevyn Aucoin

What will you choose today?

Will you choose to feel life?

Or to deny it?

To choose it, means to embrace all of it.

To let all of it be so.

love & freedom

may 5

"If your compassion does not include yourself, it is incomplete."
-Jack Kornfield

Today, show yourself compassion.

A sweet word.

A gift.

Forgiveness.

Comfort.

love & compassion

may 6

"We must walk consciously only part way toward our goal, and then leap in the dark to our success."
-Henry David Thoreau

Some days you may walk consciously.

Some days you may leap into the unknown.

Both are on the path to success.

Just keep moving.

love & leaping

may 7

"To slow down is a power move."
-Amy Cuddy

Today, slow it all way down.

Breathe.

Be.

Witness what is so right now.

What is so from here?

love & power

may 8

"I have fallen in love with the imagination. And if you fall in love with the imagination, you understand that it is a free spirit. It will go anywhere, and it can do anything."
-Alice Walker

Your imagination has been shut down for too long.

It's been told it can't.

It's been told it is silly.

Today, set your imagination free.

Let your imagination roam.

Let it do anything it wants to.

Let it go anywhere it wants to.

Let it play.

And let yourself fall in love for a while.

love & imagining

may 9

"Choose to focus your time, energy and conversation around people who inspire you, support you and help you to grow you into your happiest, strongest, wisest self."
-Karen Salmansohn

Where will you focus your time?

Where will you focus your energy?

Where will you focus your conversation?

You get to choose.

Let me say this again, because it's easy to forget...

YOU get to choose.

love & growing

may 10

"Laughter is inner jogging."
 -Norman Cousins

Do you not feel like EXERCISING today?

Well, guess what?

Today's your lucky day.

'Cause I'm here to tell you that laughter counts!

Be sure to get your inner jog in today.

Your body and heart will thank you.

love & laughter

may 11

"Do your little bit of good where you are; it's those little bits of good put together that overwhelm the world."
–Desmond Tutu

The suffering this planet sees and has seen threatens to break the heart. It can feel very intense and overwhelming. It can be easy to long to turn away. To shut it out. To shut down.

Desmond Tutu's words of wisdom above are a great comfort - especially on days when the world's suffering is especially present.

These words are a comfort - and a call to action. It needn't be massive, or painful, or add suffering to take on. It can, in fact, be "a little bit". When we do this "little bit" of good, rather than being overwhelmed, WE overwhelm.

We bring love to the world through each bit of good we do. That is our job. To do our bit of good. That is all that's needed.

Together, that's all that's needed.

love & action

may 12

"It does not matter how slowly you go as long as you do not stop."
-Confucius

Sometimes, it can feel very tempting to just throw up our hands and quit.

Work, projects, goals, relationships... you name it, the time you want to quit will come.

When it does, know how natural this is.

And remember that the #1 key to success is just this - to keep going, no matter how small or slow the steps are - to not give up.

It doesn't matter the speed you proceed.

Trust the speed you are going.

Your only job is to not give up - to take one small step each day forward.

So simple.

love & one step at a time

may 13

"I learned that courage was not the absence of fear, but the triumph over it. The brave man is not he who does not feel afraid, but he who conquers that fear."
-Nelson Mandela

I've spent a lot of years afraid. Sometimes, I've been afraid to leave the house. Sometimes, I've been afraid to speak. Sometimes, I've been afraid to answer the phone. Sometimes, I've been afraid to sit in the quiet.

Courage is not making the fear go away.

Courage is doing the thing anyway.

Sometimes courage doesn't look like much from the outside.

Sometimes the size of courage can only be truly appreciated from within.

You know what it takes to keep going.

I honor the courage in you, today.

love & courage

may 14

"Try to be a rainbow in someone else's cloud."
-Maya Angelou

Rainbows bring:
    Color

    Forgiveness

    Miracles

    Smiles

Today, bring some rainbows to someone who's feeling cloudy.

Pro Tip: If YOU feel cloudy, it still works.
It becomes a double rainbow.

love & rainbows

may 15

"The sky is always there for me, while my life has been going through many, many changes. When I look up the sky, it gives me a nice feeling, like looking at an old friend."
–Yoko Ono

Life brings many changes.

And many constants.

Expect the changes.

Rely on the constants.

When the changes feel too much, cozy up to the constants, like you would a dear old friend.

love & the sky

may 16

"When we give ourselves the chance to let go of all our tension, the body's natural capacity to heal itself can begin to work."
-Thich Nhat Hanh

Today, find ways to let your body relax and release tension.

Let go.

Make room for healing.

Breathe. Sleep. Move. Swim. Dance. Stretch. Be.

love & healing

may 17

"When you dance, your purpose is not to get to a certain place on the floor. It's to enjoy each step along the way."
-Wayne Dyer

Let today be a dance.

There's no place to get to.

Enjoy each step along the way.

love & being

may 18

*"I am my own experiment.
I am my own work of art."*
-Madonna

You get to experiment.

You get to play.

You get to create.

You get to BE a work of art.

love & creation

may 19

"There are two great days in a person's life - the day we are born and the day we discover why."
-William Barclay

My life purpose is LOVE.

What is yours?

What is your 'why'?

It needn't be complex.

It needn't be grand.

Or maybe it always is...

love & purpose

may 20

"Do things for people not because of who they are or what they do in return, but because of who you are."
-Harold S. Kushner

Kindness need not be reserved for the deserving.

Kindness need not be reserved for the rewarding.

Let kindness flow from your kindest heart.

It doesn't matter who it's for.

It matters who it's from.

(((((YOU.)))))

love & kindness

may 21

"Difficulties are meant to rouse, not discourage. The human spirit is to grow strong by conflict."
–William Ellery Channing

Avoiding conflict is not necessarily the way of the spirit. Or the way of peace.

Ewww.... such annoying news!

To face conflict and difficulties - to sit with the discomfort and unease - may be the greatest spiritual practice of all.

There is, perhaps, no greater means to develop the human spirit.

love & strength

may 22

"It is good to love many things, for therein lies the true strength, and whosoever loves much performs much, and can accomplish much, and what is done in love is well done."
–Vincent Van Gogh

For today, let yourself love many things.

You need not be selective.

Love.

Appreciate.

Get all starry-eyed.

love & loving all the things

may 23

"If ever you find yourself doubting you can make it through a challenge, simply think back to everything you've overcome in the past."
-Karen Salmansohn

Big challenge?

Overwhelming situation?

Stop.

Step back.

List out all that you've made it through.

Let go of the HOW.
("How will I ever get through this?")

And remember the WHO.
("Who I am.")

love & remembrance

may 24

"Self love is creating space in your life to heal your body and mind."
-Yung Pueblo

Self love does not happen by accident.

It happens with intention.

Look at the week ahead and create space for healing.

Set aside time for you.

Time to rest.

Time to do things that light you up.

Time to do no-things.

Time to dream and space out.

Time to talk, create, appreciate, and play.

love & healing

may 25

"Music is a higher revelation than all wisdom and philosophy."
-Ludwig van Beethoven

Infuse your day with music.

Listen to the music's wisdom.

Feel music's truth.

All shall be revealed.

love & music

may 26

"You are the sky – everything else it's just the weather."
-Pema Chodron

Some days it all feels too much.

On days like this, remember that "it" is just the weather.

It's not who you are.

It's not the big picture.

It's the details. It's the weather.

It too shall pass.

You are so much more than that.

Remember who you are.

love & majesty

may 27

"Compassionate people ask for what they need. They say no when they need to, and when they say yes, they mean it. They're compassionate because their boundaries keep them out of resentment."
–Brené Brown

It is easy to equate compassion with saying 'YES, I WILL HELP YOU' to everyone who requests it. It is easy to equate compassion with not being a bother - not troubling others - for what we need or want.

How 'bout we switch that up in our heads.

It is compassionate to say 'NO' when you need to.

It is compassionate to say 'YES' when you mean it.

It is compassionate to ask for what you need or want.

It is compassionate to be open to receive what you need or want.

love & compassion

may 28

"The only way to deal with an unfree world is to become so absolutely free that your very existence is an act of rebellion."
–Albert Camus

So many "Must-do's".

So many "Have-to's".

Do you really?

Do you *really*???

Remember how very free you are.

Really.

love & freedom

may 29

"Any action is often better than no action, especially if you have been stuck in an unhappy situation for a long time. If it is a mistake, at least you learn something, in which case it's no longer a mistake."
-Eckhart Tolle

What situation in your life do you feel stuck in?

Today, take some action in that area.

Big or small.

Clean or messy.

Shake things up.

Do a thing.

Even if it's a mistake (aka a miss-take) it's one step towards where you want to be.

love & action

may 30

"It's *never too late to become who you want to be.*"
-F. Scott Fitzgerald

Who do you want to be when you grow up?

It's never too late to dream a new dream or begin a new beginning.

What will you dream and be today?

love & being

may 31

"No, this is not the beginning of a new chapter in my life; this is the beginning of a new book! That first book is already closed, ended, and tossed into the seas; this new book is newly opened, has just begun! Look, it is the first page!
And it is a beautiful one!"
-C. JoyBell C.

Ahhh, not just a new chapter.

Today we begin an entirely new book!

The old one has ended.

It is blessed and released.

What will be written on this first page?

What beauty will you witness?

What will you receive?

What will you explore?

love & adventure

june

june 1

"The sun is a daily reminder that we too can rise again from the darkness, that we too can shine our own light."
-S. Ajna

When you feel in shadow, you may wait for a light to appear.

Remember, there is light in you already.

Breathe in.

Breathe out.

Your breath fans the spark.

love & your very own light

june 2

"The fact that I can plant a seed and it becomes a flower, share a bit of knowledge and it becomes another's, smile at someone and receive a smile in return, are to me continual spiritual exercises."
–Leo Buscaglia

Each day we have a chance to play with spirit.

To share a story is to share spirit.

To smile at another is to share spirit.

To plant a seed and nurture it to grow is to nurture spirit.

There is nothing small about these "small" things.

These are the grandest spiritual practices of all.

love & spirit

june 3

"Adopt the pace of nature:
her secret is patience."
-Ralph Waldo Emerson

Ewwww, icky, icky patience.

Even the word patience makes me want to throw things.

I want it RIGHT NOW!!!!

Such toddleresque tantrums cause mucho suffering.

The great secret of nature is patience.

By showing patience, we magnify the love we show for ourselves and others.

Patience, love.

Patience, LOVE.

Where are you throwing tantrums - that you could shine the light of patience on?

What could be happening right on time?

love & patience

june 4

"Music is a higher revelation than all wisdom and philosophy."
-Ludwig van Beethoven

Infuse your day with music.

Listen to the music's wisdom.

Feel music's truth.

All shall be revealed.

love & music

june 5

"What happens is not as important as how you react to what happens."
-Ellen Glasgow

Today, pay special attention to:

1) The things that happen.

2) How you react to the things that happened.

Recognize these are two very separate things.

Your reaction includes:

Your thoughts about the thing that happened.

Your physical response.

Your emotional response.

The action you choose to take.

Notice.

You are more powerful than you know.

love & curiosity

june 6

"Security is mostly a superstition. It does not exist in nature, nor do the children of men as a whole experience it. Avoiding danger is no safer in the long run than outright exposure. Life is either a daring adventure, or nothing."
–Helen Keller

If we expect security and safety in this life, we are setting ourselves up for deep disappointment.

Toddlers learning to walk fall. They don't just fall once. They fall over and over. It's gotta hurt. And yet, they do it. They have the drive to learn. They have the drive to step out, despite the danger.

Do you have this drive?

This drive is LOVE.

This drive is in our NATURE.

love & adventure

june 7

"Once we believe in ourselves, we can risk curiosity, wonder, spontaneous delight, or any experience that reveals the human spirit."
-e.e. cummings

Don't believe?

No worries.

I have belief in you.

You can borrow some of mine.

Breathe into this belief and be curious, wonder, and delight in what is.

love & experience

june 8

"We will be more successful in all our endeavors if we can let go of the habit of running all the time, and take little pauses to relax and re-center ourselves. And we'll also have a lot more joy in living."
-Thich Nhat Hanh

Your mission today, should you choose to accept, is to find little pauses within your day to Relax and Re-center.

That's right.

By letting go of the running and busy-ness, by adding pauses to relax and re-center, we create space for clarified action.

Space to receive success.

Is your busy-ness and your hurry pushing your success and joy away?

Consider making space for something different.

love & little pauses

june 9

"Every story I create, creates me.
I write to create myself."
-Octavia E. Butler

Each day, we create our lives.

Such power!

We can re-create our lives each day.

What story will you write for yourself today?

love & creation

june 10

"The practice of forgiveness is our most important contribution to the healing of the world."
-Marianne Williamson

It is easy to stand in judgment.

What if it could be just as easy to stand in forgiveness? I say STAND in forgiveness, for true forgiveness is not passive. It is active.

It can feel like you are standing in a roaring wind.

It is so much easier to curse the wind and run away.

But what if forgiveness was the key to every thing?

What if this was the key to the healing of the world?

Some things are worth standing in the roaring wind for.

love & forgiveness

june 11

"As I get older, the more I stay focused on the acceptance of myself and others, and choose compassion over judgment and curiosity over fear."
-Tracee Ellis Ross

When we feel judgment today, practice compassion.

When we feel fear today, practice curiosity.

When we feel rejection today, practice acceptance.

love & curiosity

june 12

"Love yourself for who you are, and trust me, if you are happy from within, you are the most beautiful person, and your smile is your best asset."
-Ileana D'Cruz

What are 10 things that you love about yourself?

Write them down.

For real.

Write them down now.

I know you got 10.

Read them back to yourself.

Feel yourself smile.

You are a treasure.

YOU are a TREASURE.

love & happiness

june 13

"Humans are amphibians - half spirit and half animal. As spirits they belong to the eternal world, but as animals they inhabit time."
-C. S. Lewis

As a human being, we inhabit time and eternity.

It is a common experience to get lost in one or the other.

Today, be sure to inhabit both.

love & eternity

june 14

"Curiosity is one of the great secrets of happiness."
-Bryant H. McGill

Today, be curious.

How does it work?

What will it do?

Who will you meet?

Why are they here?

Why are YOU here?

Go easy.

Be playful.

love & curiosity

june 15

"Be pleasant until 10 o'clock in the morning and the rest of the day will take care of itself."
-Elbert Hubbard

Try this experiment.

Be pleasant until 10 in the morning.

If it feels like an effort, put the effort in.

Then relax and see what happens.

love & pleasure

june 16

"Gratitude is riches.
Complaint is poverty."
-Doris Day

Complaints are bankrupt.

Today, try being a no-complaint zone.

No complaints issued - zip it!

No complaints heard - walk away!

Let gratitude flow through your mind, your
heart, your words.

Each word, thought, and feeling of gratitude
makes you richer.

love & gratitude

june 17

"I only went out for a walk and finally concluded to stay out till sundown, for going out, I found, was really going in."
-John Muir

Almost everything feels better when you get outside.

Make some time today to go out.

To breathe the air.

To look at the sky.

To walk the earth.

By going out today, you will find a sure path in.

love & being

june 18

"A human being is a part of the whole, called by us "Universe", a part limited in time and space. He experiences himself, his thoughts and feelings as something separated from the rest, a kind of optical delusion of his consciousness. This delusion is a kind of prison for us, restricting us to our personal desires and to affection for a few persons nearest to us. Our task must be to free ourselves from this prison by widening our circle of compassion to embrace all living creatures and the whole of nature in its beauty."
-Albert Einstein

Our separation is a delusion. A delusion that keeps us isolated, confused, limited. It makes life seem very hard. Embrace the whole of nature today. Shift from doing to being with.

Feel the beauty found through widening your circle of compassion.

love & beauty

june 19

"Daring to set boundaries is about having the courage to love ourselves, even when we risk disappointing others."
-Brené Brown

Setting boundaries does not mean we do not love others.

It means we love them.

It means we love us.

They might be disappointed.

And we might feel very uncomfortable.

It is an act of bold, courageous love.

love & courage

june 20

"*I will not play tug o' war. I'd rather play hug o' war. Where everyone hugs instead of tugs, Where everyone giggles and rolls on the rug, Where everyone kisses, and everyone grins, and everyone cuddles, and everyone wins.*"
-Shel Silverstein

What are you fighting in life?

Are there places in life that you are playing tug o' war - where you could drop the battle?

Could you bring some laughter?

Could you bring a grin?

Is it even possible that everyone could win?

love & winning

june 21

"We're all a little weird. And life is a little weird. And when we find someone whose weirdness is compatible with ours, we join up with them and fall into mutually satisfying weirdness—and call it love—true love."
-Robert Fulghum

Chances are, there's going to be some weird things going on today.

We can judge others for it.

We may judge ourselves for it.

Today, rather than pushing the weird away, can we accept the weird for what it is?

Part of our spark and inner light?

Seek partners that share your weirdness.

Friends, family, partners, spouses.

These are our true loves.

love & happiness

june 22

"Always laugh when you can, it is cheap medicine."
-Lord Byron

Get your laughter in today.

Spread joy.

Outside of you.

And inside of you.

Heal outside of you.

And inside of you.

love & laughter

june 23

"A gentle word, a kind look, a good-natured smile can work wonders and accomplish miracles."
-William Hazlitt

Want miracles?

Practice kindness.

Practice smiling.

Practice gentleness.

Go easy.

love & wonder

june 24

"I'm going to do what feeds my soul."
-Elijah Cummings

What feeds your soul?

Write these things down.

Make room for these soul-nourishing things today.

((And every day after.))

love & nourishment

june 25

"Picking up the pieces is required to solve any puzzle, especially the one called life."
-Cornell Lewis

Life can be puzzling.

Sometimes, we can stand in the mix of it all and be very unclear of where to go.

Sometimes, with the help of the big picture, we can start to put the puzzle together.

And sometimes, even if we can't see the big picture, we can start by picking up the pieces, and placing matching edges together, doing the next most logical and aligned step.

Whether you can see the big picture or not, the puzzle is solvable.

And you can start by picking up one piece at a time.

love & mystery

june 26

"So much has been given to me, I have no time to ponder over that which has been denied."
-Helen Keller

When we focus on what we have lost,
we will lose more.

When we focus on what we have been denied,
more will be kept from us.

When we focus on what we have been given,
more will be given.

What we focus on, we will receive more of.

What will you choose to focus on today?

love & gratitude

june 27

"I'm the bionic woman. I have a very strong constitution, and I take excruciatingly good care of myself."
-Angela Lansbury

Do yourself a favor and listen to the wise Angela.

Take EXCRUCIATINGLY good care of yourself today.

And all the days.

Be outrageous in your love and care for yourself.

love & strength

june 28

"Ordinary riches can be stolen; real riches cannot. In your soul are infinitely precious things that cannot be taken from you."
-Oscar Wilde

What riches reside in your soul?

Get quiet, be still, and breathe into these precious things.

These riches can never be taken from you.

And they are easily grown.

Breath by breath.

Thought by thought.

Smile by smile.

love & riches

june 29

"Find out who you are and be that person. That's what your soul was put on this Earth to be. Find that truth, live that truth and everything else will come."
-Ellen DeGeneres

Who are you?

What is your truth?

Be that.

Live that.

Everything else will fall into place.

Promise.

love & truth

june 30

"For every minute you remain angry, you give up sixty seconds of peace of mind."
-Ralph Waldo Emerson

Being angry robs us of our time and peace.

In effect it can make us - lose our mind!

Cool thing this, we can feel anger, and free it, and get back to peace.

It is within our power.

love & peace

july

july 1

"Learning to treat ourselves lovingly may at first feel like a dangerous experiment."
-Sharon Salzberg

Mmmmm.... How can you show yourself exquisite LOVE today?

OUCH! Did that sound Weird? Odd? Scary? Unusual? Unnecessary?

Even dangerous?

That's what we're talking about! Soak up that beautiful love. You deserve it, sweetheart.

love & courage

july 2

"Do not grow old, no matter how long you live. Never cease to stand like curious children before the Great Mystery into which we were born."
-Albert Einstein

BEHOLD! There is a whole, grand, mystery-of-a-day ahead of you!

What if you were seeing it all for the first time?

Do you know that you actually are?

Be curious. Explore. Be surprised. Be captivated.

The world's a mystery. And you are too. A beautiful, exquisite, captivating one.

love & curiosity

july 3

"Sometimes the most important thing in a whole day is the rest we take between two deep breaths."
-Etty Hillesum

Breathe.

Rest.

Breathe.

Sometimes, that's all we need.

love & breath

july 4

"You must love in such a way that the person you love feels free."
-Thich Nhat Hanh

YES! It is such a gift, a blessing to your partner, your friends, your children, your family, to be loved in a way that we all feel free.

It is an even grander gift to love YOURSELF in such a way that YOU feel free.

Let go of the shoulds, the self-judgment, the make-wrong, the prisons, the enclosures, the limits, and the expectations you set for yourself.

You are so beautiful and needed in the world, just as you are. You are FREE.

love & freedom

july 5

"Truly accepting your love nature requires you to relinquish all the stories and pretenses you've created about yourself."
-Gabrielle Bernstein

Just for today, can you know nothing about yourself?

You aren't your past, your fears, your successes, your challenges, your passions, your excuses, your reasons, your heartbreaks, your loves.

You are you.

Love who you are in this moment. No stories or explanations required.

love & acceptance

july 6

"He didn't quit his day job to follow his dream; he just folded his dream into his everyday life. He wanted to raise goats, so he acquired some goats...When my father grew curious about things, he pursued them."
–Elizabeth Gilbert

What do you want to learn more about? What do you want to discover? What have you always wanted to create?

What have you been dreaming of and holding off "until"?

How can you fold this dream into your everyday life?

How can you start today?

love & creation

july 7

"The more clearly we can focus our attention on the wonders and realities of the universe about us, the less taste we shall have for destruction."
-Rachel Carson

The universe we live in is brimming with so much wonder and infinite miracles.

When we wish to throw in the towel...when we wish to throw up our hands...when we wish to crush...when we wish to throw out....when we wish to destroy...

Let us open our eyes and dwell on the mysteries that surround us.

Each breath. Each step. Each star. Each flower. Each grain of sand. All miracles.

love & wonder

july 8

"The presence of Fear is a sure sign you are trusting in your own strength."
-A Course in Miracles

Are you afraid?

Breathe deep.

You need not face it alone. You need not rely on your own strength.

Share your fear, be open, stretch out your arms, and be ready to receive. You have more on your side than you know.

love & open arms

july 9

"Nothing will work unless you do."
-Maya Angelou

Today, work for YOU. Take a step forward today towards your dream. A baby step or a giant step. Just make sure it is one that you have not taken before.

The Universe is watching.

It will see where you are walking and create pathways for your feet to tread.

But you need to step forward to find them.

love & action

july 10

"Goodbyes are only for those who love with their eyes. Because for those who love with heart and soul there is no such thing as separation."
-Rumi

Who have you loved and lost?

Close your eyes.

Remember.

Call them to your mind.

Call them into your heart.

They are not lost. You are not separate.

They are with you.

love & a million more hellos

july 11

"I have not failed. I've just found 10,000 ways that will not work."
-Thomas A. Edison

Have you failed?

Congratulations! That means you stuck your head out there and TRIED.

Keep at it! Keep failing! Keep trying! The next time it could be the time you land on solid ground and it "works".

It might have even "worked" already!

Don't walk away. Don't leave your baby dream just as it's expanding.

Keep going.

I can't wait to see your dream light up the world.

love & tenacity

july 12

"Through my love for you, I want to express my love for the whole cosmos, the whole of humanity, and all beings. By living with you, I want to learn to love everyone and all species. If I succeed in loving you, I will be able to love everyone and all species on earth...
This is the real message of love."
-Thich Nhat Hanh

Is there someone in your life who drives you completely batty?

Sometimes, we choose to walk away.

Sometimes, we choose to find a higher purpose.

Sometimes, we choose a little of both.

Just for today, love that crazy, maddening soul a little more. Whether you are in their presence or not.

love & more love

july 13

"Loving yourself isn't vanity, it's sanity."
-Katrina Meyer

Seriously.

You are allowed to love yourself.

You are allowed to take care of yourself.

To not love yourself is totally cuckoo.

You are a miracle.

How could we NOT love you?

How could YOU not love you?

love & sanity

july 14

"It takes courage to say yes to rest and play in a culture where exhaustion is seen as a status symbol."
–Brené Brown

"How are you?"

"Busy" / "Tired"

These are the easiest and most expected responses.

Being busy and tired is code for "hard worker", "good work ethic", "important".

It takes courage to live differently.

What if we created a culture where we are actually enjoying each beautiful day we have been given on this earth, taking delight in giving our body the rest and play that it craves, loving each moment so fully that we can be awake when awake?

love & courage

july 15

"Being in union with the energy of the Universe is like an awesome dancer where you trust your partner so much that you just surrender to the beat of the music."
-Gabrielle Bernstein

My darling, just for today, can you surrender to the music of the Universe?

As an experiment, let go of controlling, of figuring it all out, of knowing how.

Keep stepping, keep moving, and see where this most awesome dancer of a Universe will take you.

love & surrender

july 16

"Smile in the mirror. Do that every morning and you'll start to see a big difference in your life."
-Yoko Ono

Look in the mirror, honey, you're beautiful!

Keep looking until you smile.

Sometimes smiles leap out.

Sometimes smiles take persistence.

Persist.

It's worth it.

love & smiles

july 17

"I err whenever my attachment to a particular outcome seduces me into trying to manage Spirit. When I'm wise enough to step aside or, better yet, step into the "flow", I succeed beyond my expectations."
–Travis Twomey

Please God, let me win the lottery! Let me get this job! Let me get this girl!

We might be certain that having a thing is the best possible outcome for us - and anything else is a failure, a loss, a defeat.

Step aside.

Yes, dream. Wish for things. Plan for things. Pray for things.

But step aside. Let it be. Let Spirit work.

Your failure, loss or defeat may lead to success beyond your wildest expectations.

love & flow

july 18

"When you plant lettuce, if it does not grow well, you don't blame the lettuce. You look for reasons it is not doing well. It may need fertilizer, or more water, or less sun. You never blame the lettuce. Yet if we have problems with our friends or family, we blame the other person. But if we know how to take care of them, they will grow well, like the lettuce. Blaming has no positive effect at all, nor does trying to persuade using reason and argument. That is my experience. No blame, no reasoning, no argument, just understanding. If you understand, and you show that you understand, you can love, and the situation will change."
-Thich Nhat Hanh

Just for today, don't blame the lettuce.

love & reason

july 19

"It's one of the greatest gifts you can give yourself, to forgive. Forgive everybody."
-Maya Angelou

Who can you forgive today?

Whether it's big, small, someone else, or yourself.

Forgiveness is always a personal gift to yourself.

The bigger the challenge, the bigger the gift.

love & forgiveness

july 20

"The best way to find yourself is to lose yourself in the service of others."
-Mahatma Gandhi

What act of service can you share with the world today?

Feel like you have nothing to give?

A smile to a stranger, a kind word, a prayer, a note of gratitude. The act of sitting and listening for 5 minutes.

These acts may seem small.

They are anything but small.

love & service

july 21

"Where the Spirit does not work with the hand there is no art."
-Leonardo Da Vinci

Are you trying to make your hands do all the work - without letting Spirit in for the assist?

Are you relying on Spirit to save you - instead of taking action?

Let today be a work of art. Take action while trusting that it's not all on you. You got some powerful backup.

love & spirit

july 22

"Let the beauty of what you love be what you do."
-Rumi

Today, spend time doing something you love.

Doing what you love is an exquisitely beautiful gift to the world.

love & beauty

july 23

"People usually consider walking on water or in thin air a miracle. But I think the real miracle is not to walk either on water or in thin air, but to walk on earth. Every day we are engaged in a miracle which we don't even recognize: a blue sky, white clouds, green leaves, the black, curious eyes of a child—our own two eyes. All is a miracle."
-Thich Nhat Hanh

What miracles will you recognize today?

Remember.

You are a miracle, too.

love & miracles

july 24

"Your work is going to fill a large part of your life, and the only way to be truly satisfied is to do what you believe is great work. And the only way to do great work is to love what you do. If you haven't found it yet, keep looking. Don't settle. As with all matters of the heart, you'll know when you find it."
-Steve Jobs

Have you found your great work?

If the answer is YES, CELEBRATE!

Embrace the find - even when it feels challenging, impossible or ridiculous. Honor that you didn't settle - that you sought it out - and that you listened to your heart.

If you have not found it, do not despair! Or settle! What can you do today to explore, to look, to seek the work you love, your great work? It could be just two steps around the corner. Keep your eyes and heart open!

love & work

july 25

"Forgive me my nonsense, as I also forgive the nonsense of those that think they talk sense."
–Robert Frost

Is it just me, or are you presented with a whole bunch of nonsense on a daily basis?

Sometimes, at least for me, the nonsense is coming out of my own face!

But, it made sense in my head....

Maybe their nonsense made sense in their head, too.

Today let's forgive the nonsense.

love & nonsense

july 26

"We know what the world wants from us. We know we must decide whether to stay small, quiet and uncomplicated or allow ourselves to grow as big, loud and complex as we were made to be."
-Glennon Doyle

Today, let yourself be as big, loud and complex as you were made to be.

love & complexity

july 27

"To love yourself right now, just as you are, is to give yourself heaven. Don't wait until you die. If you wait, you die now. If you love, you live now."
-Alan Cohen

No fair waiting.

Love that beautiful, magnificent, creative, a-little-wild (or a lot), a-little-crazy (or a lot), sometimes scared, sometimes forgetful, late or early, sometimes stingy, sometimes generous, person you are right now.

Love all of you.

This is heaven.

love & heaven

july 28

"At times our own light goes out and is rekindled by a spark from another person. Each of us has cause to think with deep gratitude of those who have lit the flame within us."
-Albert Schweitzer

Has your light gone out?

Stop and pause.

Can you be open to it being rekindled?

Take a few moments to be open to receive.

See what happens...

Has your light gone out before?

Who has gotten your light going again?

Will you express your gratitude today?

Perhaps you could be their spark today.

love & spark

july 29

"The first step toward discarding a scarcity mentality involves giving thanks for everything that you have."
-Wayne Dyer

Oh, my, how guilty are we of seeing what we lack, rather than what we have?!?

I see the dirty bathroom sink. The stinky litter box. The dirty laundry on the floor. The mold on the roof.

Today, I will see and give thanks for the roof that works perfectly! The indoor plumbing! The adorable kitty cats. My daughter. My son.

Only when we are grateful for what we have, can we possibly experience abundance.

And we may discover, along the way, that what we have is way, way, WAY more than we need.

love & gratitude

july 30

"To be beautiful means to be yourself.
You don't need to be accepted by others.
You need to accept yourself."
-Thich Nhat Hanh

Hey, beautiful!

The world needs you to be yourself today!

It might not accept you, but it NEEDS you, as you are.

You are exquisite. You are perfect. You are beautiful. You are just what the world needs.

love & beauty

july 31

"Accept that you have the right to be happy. You have the right to thrive, shine and succeed. Give yourself the gift of opening your mind to a world beyond what you have been taught to believe in."
-Gabrielle Bernstein

What if things weren't the way they had to be?

What if things weren't the way you've been taught?

Today, practice noticing when you think: "it couldn't" / "if only" / "wouldn't that be great."

What if what you wanted was actually completely possible?

What if thriving, shining, and succeeding was entirely welcomed?

Today, even if you feel silly believing, act AS IF what you want is possible. You might just find that it is.

love & surprises

august

august 1

"We all have 2 choices:
We can make a living or design a life."
–Jim Rohn

Give yourself some love today.

If you were designing your life, would it be the one you are living?

If yes, celebrate! YES. CELEBRATE!

If not, give yourself some love today. What would your ideal life look like?

Sit and envision it. Write it down.

Draw it out. Create a Vision Board.

The universe has a sneaky way of helping us create what we actually desire.

Let's show it what we desire.

love & creation

august 2

"I don't have to chase extraordinary moments to find happiness – it's right in front of me if I'm paying attention and practicing gratitude."
–Brené Brown

Close your eyes.

What are three things you are grateful for right now?

Open your eyes - and keep them open - for things to be grateful for.

The simple moments turn extraordinary through this. This is the path to happiness. It's not what we have. It's what we see.

love & gratitude

august 3

"I have learned silence from the talkative, toleration from the intolerant, and kindness from the unkind; yet, strange, I am ungrateful to those teachers."
-Khalil Gibran

Some of the most important lessons in our lives feel truly awful.

Gratitude for that comes hard.

Tip-toe a bit more into gratitude for the talkative, the intolerant, the unkind.

Be grateful for who they've made you today.

And if you can't, that's ok. Kahlil Gibran wasn't either. And he was pretty genius.

love & learning

august 4

"It is a happy talent to know how to play."
-Ralph Waldo Emerson

Ah ha! Today we play!

Play your way to the elevator. Remember how fun it was to push the buttons?

Play your way with the laundry. Remember how fun it was to throw clothes in?

Play your way in the rain. Remember how fun it was to splash in puddles?

Play your way to the car. Remember how fun it was to hop over cracks in the sidewalk?

If you have forgotten how to play, find a 3 year old and hang out with them.

Playing is NOT a waste of time. It is a talent. Being able to play is necessary for creativity and true intelligence. This is what the world desperately needs.

love & play

august 5

"Sleep is the best meditation."
–The 14th Dalai Lama Tenzin Gyatso

Today, take a nap.

And if anyone gives you grief, tell them the Dalai Lama told you to!

Divine, delicious, exquisite sleep.

love & slumber

august 6

"Let my soul smile through my heart and my heart smile through my eyes, that I may scatter rich smiles in sad hearts."
-Paramahansa Yogananda

Our souls can smile through anything - even sadness and heartbreak.

Be that smile that warms a heart.

Have that heart that lets a smile in.

love & smiles

august 7

"At the deepest level, there is no giver, no gift, and no recipient... only the universe rearranging itself."
-Jon Kabat-Zinn

Some days we are in the position to give. Some days we are in the position to receive. Wildly, in both we are giving and receiving.

In giving we receive, in receiving we give.

Wherever you find yourself today, be grateful and trust the universe to rearrange itself with its wisdom.

love & trust

august 8

"Creativity requires the courage to let go of certainties."
-Erich Fromm

Today, let go of knowing.

Let go of knowing how things will go, what will work or what can't work, who is right or who is wrong, what is stupid and what is smart.

Have the courage to let go of your certainty of 'the way things are.'

Have the courage to create room for what might not have seemed possible before.

love & courage

august 9

"If we're destroying our trees and destroying our environment and hurting animals and hurting one another and all that stuff, there's got to be a very powerful energy to fight that. I think we need more love in the world. We need more kindness, more compassion, more joy, more laughter. I definitely want to contribute to that."
-Ellen Degeneres

Today, let your sole job on earth be to spread more love in the world.

Whether it be through kindness, compassion, joy or laughter, spread love.

love & laughter

august 10

"Breathing in, I calm my body.
Breathing out, I smile.
Dwelling in the present moment,
I know this is a wonderful moment."
-Thich Nhat Hanh

Stop in this moment from recycling the past or formulating the future.

Breathe and be in this moment.

Experience the wonder of what is.

love & wonder

august 11

"The most difficult times for many of us are the ones we give ourselves."
-Pema Chödrön

Oh, how we beat ourselves up!

Today, let yourself off the hook.

You did your best.

You are doing your best.

You are forgiven.

love & more love

august 12

"For beautiful eyes, look for the good in others; for beautiful lips, speak only words of kindness; and for poise, walk with the knowledge that you are never alone."
-Audrey Hepburn

Embody beauty.

Walk in kindness.

See the light in others.

See the light in you.

Your beauty will be more brilliant each day.

You stunner, you.

love & beauty

august 13

"It does not matter how slowly you go as long as you don't stop."
-Confucious

It's okay to go slow today.

And you never know - even a little step might bring you over the finish line.

love & baby steps

august 14

"It's not our job to play judge and jury, to determine who is worthy of our kindness and who is not. We just need to be kind, unconditionally and without ulterior motive, even - or rather, especially - when we'd prefer not to be."
-Josh Radnor

Be kind.

Expect nothing.

Judge nothing.

Give your mind a rest.

love & rest

august 15

"Each day holds a surprise. But only if we expect it can we see, hear, or feel it when it comes to us. Let's not be afraid to receive each day's surprise, whether it comes to us as sorrow or as joy. It will open a new place in our hearts, a place where we can welcome new friends and celebrate more fully our shared humanity."
-Henri Nouwen

Wait for it...

What brand new discovery will you come upon today?

Eyes open.

Heart open.

Welcome!

love & surprises

august 16

*"Darkness cannot drive out darkness;
only light can do that. Hate cannot drive
out hate; only love can do that."*
-Martin Luther King, Jr.

When we look out and all seems dark,
do not despair.

Be the light.

Be the love.

Even "just" one person can spark the love and
turn the tides.

Be the one.

love & light

august 17

"And forget not that the earth delights to feel your bare feet and the winds long to play with your hair."
-Khalil Gibran

Walk on the earth.

Let your bare feet feel the ground.

Let the wind play with your hair.

Breathe and Be.

That which delights the earth is sure to delight you, too.

love & being

august 18

"Your attitude is like a box of crayons that color your world. Constantly color your picture gray, and your picture will always be bleak. Try adding some bright colors to the picture by including humor, and your picture begins to lighten up."
–Allen Klein

Today, pick a bright color.

Laugh with it.

Laugh over it.

Laugh through it.

love & laughter

august 19

"Walk as if you are kissing the Earth with your feet."
-Thich Nhat Hanh

Today, walk for the sake of walking.

Not to leave where you were. Or to go where you are going.

To walk for walking's sake.

To touch the earth for the earth's sake.

Imagine you could kiss the earth with your feet.

You might just feel a little giddy.

love & kisses

august 20

"Those who bring sunshine to the lives of others cannot keep it from themselves."
-James Matthew Barrie

If you are reading this, it means you've brought sunshine into my life.

Thank you.

Shine on, beautiful.

Shine on.

love & sun

august 21

"The whole idea of compassion is based on a keen awareness of the interdependence of all these living beings, which are all part of one another, and all involved in one another."
-Thomas Merton

Today, look closely. See how much we rely on others. See how much they rely on us. See how we are all a part of one another.

All the people that brought your dinner to your plate. All the people that brought you the movie you watch. All the people that drive you to work.

Independence is a myth.

See all the people that make your "independence" possible. See how you make "independence" possible for so many others.

We are all a part of one another.

Compassion for another is compassion for ourselves. And the other way around, too.

love & compassion

august 22

"Yesterday is gone. Tomorrow has not yet come. We have only today. Let us begin."
-Mother Teresa

Today, you get to begin everything you've ever dreamed of.

Really.

Live it today.

love & beginnings

august 23

"The key to success is to focus our consciousness mind on things we desire, not things we fear."
-Brian Tracy

I used to wake in worry or fear of what was to come. It was a blessing when I learned that I had a choice as to whether I carried it with me or not.

It wasn't a magic poof, a chant of "FEAR DISAPPEAR", and instant bliss. It took the decision to choose love and desire.

Until one day, my thoughts were more of desire and love than of fear. The fear ratio was less. It felt like magic.

Even though it hadn't been magic, really. It had been a choice. A choice that was made over and over again. Day by day, moment by moment. A choice I keep making. A choice we get to make over and over again, regardless of what we've chosen before. Which is a bit of magic, after all.

love & desire

august 24

"The more you praise and celebrate your life, the more there is in life to celebrate."
-Oprah Winfrey

What will celebrate today?

Celebrate what you have.

Celebrate who you have.

Celebrate who you are.

Celebrate how far you've come.

And watch what you have to celebrate expand.

love & praises

august 25

"Love and Compassion are necessities, not luxuries. Without them humanity cannot survive."
–The 14th Dalai Lama Tenzin Gyatso

When we think of basic needs most of us think of food, shelter, clothing.

That's what it takes for survival.

But we also need, absolutely require, love.

Without love and kindness - both giving and receiving - we wither. We leave our bodies while they are still moving.

In this wild world, where most people are disconnected from their very humanity, we are craving love and compassion more than ever before.

Let's bring it.

love & compassion

august 26

"Make a list of what is really important to you. Embody it."
-Jon Kabat-Zinn

What is most important to you?

For me: Love. Freedom. Passion. Art. Spirit. Creative expression. My children. My family. Our mother Earth. For people to have a roof overhead and know that they are loved. Leaving the world better than I found it. My garden.

Am I embodying this list?

Are you embodying your list?

If not, no wonder you will feel out of wack.

And, how excellent it is, that once we embody our lists, life flows.

How about we do that?

love & ease

august 27

"Infuse your life with action. Don't wait for it to happen. Make it happen. Make your own future. Make your own hope. Make your own love. And whatever your beliefs, honor your creator, not by passively waiting for grace to come down from upon high, but by doing what you can to make grace happen... yourself, right now, right down here on Earth."
-Bradley Whitford

What can you make happen today?

Hope?

Love?

Honor?

Grace?

Honor your creator.

By creating.

love & action

august 28

"In dealing with those who are undergoing great suffering, if you feel "burnout" setting in, if you feel demoralized and exhausted, it is best, for the sake of everyone, to withdraw and restore yourself. The point is to have a long-term perspective."
–The 14th Dalai Lama Tenzin Gyatso

Listen to the Dalai Lama!

When you feel exhausted or you feel your spark dimming, give yourself space and time to restore.

The world needs you around for the long-term.

love & restoration

august 29

"And now that you don't have to be perfect, you can be good."
–John Steinbeck

Dear one, you don't need to be perfect.

And neither does anyone else.

Be love.

Be loved.

That is all.

love & more love

august 30

"Those who think they have no time for bodily exercise will sooner or later have to find time for illness."
–Edward Stanley

Ouch, that hurt.

Our bodies were made to move around and keep moving.

Our bodies will protest if they are not given what they need!

Give your body a gift today.

Today, even if it's 5 minutes, move your body.

Stretch, walk, play, dance, garden, jump, meander in the woods, prance, swim.

It's like kisses for the body.

love & kisses

august 31

"Find ecstasy in life; the mere sense of living is joy enough."
-Emily Dickinson

Breathe, dear one, you are alive.

Each day, each breath, each moment, can bring ecstasy and joy. If we allow it.

love & ecstasy

september

september 1

"Healing yourself is connected with healing others."
-Yoko Ono

If you find yourself needing to heal today, give yourself full permission to do so.

Set everything else aside.

Allow space for healing.

As we heal ourselves, we can know we are healing others.

love & healing

september 2

"Joy is the serious business of Heaven."
-C.S. Lewis

Each moment of joy is a moment with God.

Love it.

Laugh it.

EnJoy it.

love & joy

september 3

"To forgive is to set a prisoner free and to discover that the prisoner was you."
-Lewis B. Smedes

Forgiveness seems like it is a gift you give someone else.

Truly, it is a gift you give to yourself.

Who can you forgive today?

A new grievance or an old grievance.

New friend or old friend.

Family or that pesky person in the mirror.

Forgive for you.

love & forgiveness

september 4

"The balancing act with a good career is to achieve personal fulfillment, to contribute to society, but also to honor the four tenets of ecological sustainability, social justice, family and community."
-Shannon Hayes

A tall order?

If your work feels off, unsatisfying, a burden, check it against Shannon Hayes' guidance.

If our work does not align with our values and these things, it is not alarming if things feel 'off.'

It could mean ditching the career, but it doesn't have to. It could mean shifting towards alignment, even if "just" a small bit.

A little change in this area of your life can make a huge difference.

love & alignment

september 5

"All things share the same breath – the beast, the tree, the man... the air shares its spirit with all the life it supports."
–Chief Seattle

Stop and breathe.

It is not only your breath.

Breathe with those near, those far, the trees, our loved ones, our not-so-loved ones, and those we'll never meet.

love & air

september 6

"I actually think sadness and darkness can be very beautiful and healing."
-Duncan Sheik

We think of healing as a beautiful and good thing.

When we are outside of the experience of healing, it sounds light and easy.

Truth is, healing often brings pain with it.

If you are feeling sad today...

If you are feeling darkness today...

Perhaps you are healing something.

Even something you might not quite understand at present.

love & healing

september 7

"When another person makes you suffer, it is because he suffers deeply within himself, and his suffering is spilling over. He does not need punishment; he needs help. That's the message he is sending."
-Thich Nhat Hanh

We have all faced someone who causes suffering.

When this happens, can we see this person's suffering?

This does not mean we welcome the suffering or let it continue.

It means we look out through our own suffering to see the other person's suffering.

How will that suffering be alleviated? How will that suffering be released?

That is the way to heal one another and our planet.

love & releasing

september 8

"Give yourself permission to allow this moment to be exactly as it is, and allow yourself to be exactly as you are."
–Jon Kabat-Zinn

Allow yourself to be as you are.

Allow this day to be as it is.

That is all.

love & being

september 9

"Remember that bodily exercise, when it is well ordered, as I have said, is also prayer by means of which you can please God our Lord."
-St. Ignatius

Loving and caring for this body is a physical expression of gratitude for this incredible gift we have been given.

Stretch, walk, sashay, play, swim, and downdog as a prayer of gratitude for this magnificent, awe-inspiring life.

love & movement

september 10

"You can't stop the waves, but you can learn to surf."
-Jon Kabat-Zinn

ARGH. Problems! Changes! Miscommunications!

We often look at life's conundrums as if something is wrong.

A change or a challenge seems wrong and something to be avoided.

Well, surprise! We can't stop it.

A fully lived life has many waves.

Would you choose to give up the adventure, in favor of still water?

While living waves will show up. Even, mysteriously, in still water.

Life is weird like that.

I'll choose to surf.

love & water

september 11

"Love is patient, love is kind. It does not envy, it does not boast, it is not proud. It is not rude, it is not self-seeking, it is not easily angered, it keeps no record of wrongs. Love does not delight in evil but rejoices with the truth."
-1 Corinthians 13:1

Today, where things feel broken and where there is hurt, rather than following the lure of evil and anger, can we choose to love just a little more?

love & more love

september 12

"Obstacles are things a person sees when he takes his eyes off his goal."
-E. Joseph Cossman

Does everything seem impossible?

Too much gobbly-gook in the way of your dreams?

Stop where you are and drop all of it.

Think of your plans NOT the reasons they won't work or what would get in your way.

Picture your vision so very clearly.

Keep seeing it that clearly.

Over time, the obstacles will slip aside.

And make way for your vision.

love & vision

september 13

"Life isn't about finding yourself.
Life is about creating yourself."
–George Bernard Shaw

Trying to find yourself?

Figure out what makes you tick?

Ah ha!

Guess what...

You get to decide.

love & creation

september 14

"Life is 10% what happens to you and 90% how you react to it."
-Charles R. Swindoll

Seriously.

How will you react today?

love & possibility

september 15

"God gave us the gift of life; it is up to us to give ourselves the gift of living well."
-Voltaire

What is one thing you can do today
to live well?

love & living

september 16

"Never lose an opportunity of seeing anything beautiful, for beauty is God's handwriting."
-Ralph Waldo Emerson

Today, keep your eyes open for beauty.

Witnessing it. Living it. Creating it.

God is in all of it.

love & beauty

september 17

"Life is an adventure in forgiveness."
-Norman Cousins

When we forgive it's like putting down a heavy backpack we've been hiking with for miles.

Who will we forgive today?

Who will we ask for forgiveness today?

This forgiveness clears the way for new beginnings.

Forgiveness clears the way for grand new adventures.

Much lighter adventures.

love & freedom

september 18

"The past, the present and the future are really one: they are today."
-Harriet Beecher Stowe

Time is such a mystery.

How often are you living in the present?

Most of us spend a good amount of our days hanging out in the past.

(Past = Blaming, reliving, idealizing, savoring, regretting.)

We also spend a good amount of time in the future.

(Future = Planning, worrying, scheming, dreaming.)

Our thoughts create our nows.

You time traveller you.

You hold the reigns. You get to choose.

love & mystery

september 19

"The moment you realign with love and stop relying on your own strength, clear direction will be presented."
–Gabrielle Bernstein

Do you find yourself worrying, stressing, trying to figure out all the pieces, trying to make them all work? Does life feel like a jigsaw puzzle with a gazillion pieces that just don't seem to go together at all?

Whenever I can remember to stop it with the puzzle, sit down, and surrender....

There is a magical shift that takes place.

I somehow see clearly where the pieces are to go.

I discover there were some extra pieces that never belonged in the box.

I discover that lost pieces are found - a passerby may bring them to me - if I'm willing to accept their ideas and help.

love & magic

september 20

"While you are proclaiming peace with your lips, be careful to have it even more fully in your heart."
-St. Francis of Assisi

Cultivate peace in your mind.

Cultivate peace in your words.

Cultivate peace in your heart.

Feel the peace grow exponentially.

love & peace

september 21

"You are what your deep, driving desire is. As your desire is, so is your will. As your will is, so is your deed."
–Brihadarahyaka Upanishad

What is your deep, driving desire?

What do you really want?

Not in your head, but in your heart.

Your will and action will follow.

When I look into my heart, what I REALLY want is love and kindness and laughter and creativity and freedom.

What do YOU really want?

love & desire

september 22

"Miracles do not, in fact, break the laws of nature."
-C. S. Lewis

Dare I say it, miracles ARE the law of nature.

Expect them.

They are appearing.

(((Whether you see them or not.)))

love & miracles

september 23

"Almost everything will work again if you unplug it for a few minutes, including you."
–Anne Lamott

Amen to that.

How will you unplug today?

love & rest

september 24

"Be content with what you have,
rejoice in the way things are. When you
realize there is nothing lacking, the
whole world belongs to you."
-Lao Tzu

Today, focus on all you have.

Feel gratitude for it.

Express gratitude for it.

You are so very rich.

love & gratitude

september 25

"There are many aspects to success; material wealth is only one component... Success also includes good health, energy and enthusiasm for life, fulfilling relationships, creative freedom, emotional and psychological stability, a sense of well-being, and peace of mind."
-Deepak Chopra

In our society, success is often equated with material wealth, money in the bank, and a big paycheck.

There is nothing wrong with having financial wealth, and financial wealth can bring tremendous good, but it does not bring happiness in and of itself.

Having financial wealth does not mean that the person is fulfilled, enjoys their days, has good relationships, or sleeps well at night.

What does success mean to you?

love & success

september 26

"Abundance can be had simply by consciously receiving that which has already been given."
-Sufi saying

It is so easy to focus on what we are lacking, rather that what we have already. When we are fully grateful for what we have - and truly know the wealth we already possess - we can open up to receive what has been given.

You have been given more than you are aware of.

Are you open to receive it?

love & receiving

september 27

*"Not what we have but what we enjoy,
constitutes our abundance."*
-Epicurus

What do you have now that you are not
enjoying?

Whether it's a comfy sweater rarely worn, a
game rarely played, a talent barely utilized, or
a relationship taken for granted ... chances are
you possess an abundance that is not enjoyed
fully.

That can change today if you choose to let it.

love & enjoyment

september 28

"Both *abundance* and *lack* exist simultaneously in our lives, as parallel realities. It is always our conscious choice which secret garden we will tend...when we choose not to focus on what is missing from our lives but are grateful for the abundance that's present– love, health, family, friends, work, the joys of nature and personal pursuits that bring us pleasure– the wasteland of illusion falls away and we experience Heaven on earth."
–Sarah Ban Breathnac

What garden will you tend today?

love & gratitude

september 29

"If you look at what you have in life, you'll always have more. If you look at what you don't have in life, you'll never have enough."
-Oprah Winfrey

In a quest for abundance, many start by focusing on what they are missing and dive right into dreaming up what they want to manifest.

This quest for abundance is in itself focused on lack, because it is starting with a focus on what you don't have and what you want.

The first step towards true abundance comes through fully knowing you already live in abundance and living in gratitude for it.

love & all the gratitude

september 30

"The journey to financial freedom starts the MINUTE you decide you were destined for prosperity, not scarcity - for abundance, not lack. Isn't there a part of you that has always known that? Can you see yourself living a bounteous life - a life of more than enough? It only takes one minute to decide. Decide now."
-Mark Victor Hansen

What were you destined for?

What do you decide?

love & decisions

october

october 1

"The trees are about to show us how lovely it is to let dead things go."
–Anonymous

What dead things are you holding onto?

Are you willing to let them go?

Thank.

Bless.

Release.

love & releasing

october 2

"Beauty ... arrives in our lives unbidden, like a special grace – but without the power of our intention it will quickly disappear, covered in uninvited clutter."
-Lauren Rosenfeld & Dr. Melva Green

Today, make some way for beauty.

Clear away the clutter - physical and mental - and make space for beauty to settle in when it appears.

love & beauty

october 3

"Music has healing power. It has the ability to take people out of themselves for a few hours."
-Elton John

Music uplifts us.

Music connects us with something bigger than ourselves.

Often within an instant.

Seek out music.

Feel its healing power.

love & harmony

october 4

"When you commit to Greatness, everything unlike itself will come up to be healed."
-Barbara Stanny

Sometimes when we're up to very good, great, loving, purposeful, important things...

Everything can seem to fall apart.

Everything seems to go wrong.

Some people see these as signs to stop.

DO NOT SEE THESE AS SIGNS TO STOP.

Persevere.

Keep going.

Keep shining your light.

Your reward is just beyond the healing.

And some stuff just needs to get kicked up a bit before the healing comes.

love & greatness

october 5

"May you live every day of your life."
-Jonathan Swift

Congratulations, you are ALIVE.

But are you LIVING?

Step to it, dear one!

Do something today that lights you up.

love & living

october 6

"Turn your wounds into wisdom."
-Oprah Winfrey

What has caused you pain?

What has needed healing?

It is easy to be lost in the pain and expect more and more of it.

Today, feel the pain, while looking for the lesson.

What does this pain have to show you?

love & wisdom

october 7

"Gratitude unlocks the fullness of life. It turns what we have into enough, and more. It turns denial into acceptance, chaos to order, confusion to clarity. It can turn a meal into a feast, a house into a home, a stranger into a friend."
-Melody Beattie

This moment, think of three things you are grateful for.

Allow the feeling of gratitude to grow from a momentary thought to an expansive light that surrounds you.

Carry this gratitude through the day with each interaction, each word, each confusion, each decision.

Feel gratitude turn the key in the lock.

Feel gratitude make sense of the confusion and bring order to the chaos.

love & gratitude

october 8

"Love is the absence of judgment."
-14th *Dalai Lama Tenzin Gyatso*

When we find ourselves concerned for another, sometimes this comes with a little sidecar of judgment.

"They shouldn't be doing that."

"If only they would…"

"How can I make them change?"

"Why won't they listen?"

Just for today, when we care for another, can we care for them without a prescription for their change?

Just for today, can we love without a cautionary tale - either out loud or in our mind?

Just for today, can we try out what it feels to love without judgment?

love & more love

october 9

"You need to learn how to select your thoughts just the same way you select your clothes every day. This is a power you can cultivate. If you want to control things in your life so bad, work on the mind. That's the only thing you should be trying to control."
-Elizabeth Gilbert

Select your thoughts just as you would a pair of jeans, shirt, and sweater.

You have way more power than you realize.

Those of us who like control, often confuse the power we have. We think we can control others. But the power we really have is over ourselves.

love & power

october 10

"Walk with those seeking truth... Run from those who think they've found it."
-Deepak Chopra

Find the people who are seekers, explorers, ever curious, wanting to learn.

You can explore the world together.

love & seeking

october 11

"As you navigate through the rest of your life, be open to collaboration. Other people and other people's ideas are often better than your own. Find a group of people who challenge and inspire you, spend a lot of time with them, and it will change your life."
-Amy Poehler

The people we spend our days with make a huge impact on what we create and grow in our lives.

Who are we choosing to collaborate with in this project of life?

Who is one person you would like to invite into your life?

Reach out today - make plans this week - it will change your life.

love & collaboration

october 12

"He who lives in harmony with himself lives in harmony with the universe."
-Marcus Aurelius

Are you living in harmony with yourself?

We face a myriad of choices in a day.

Today, as choices arise, ask yourself... what choice is in harmony with you?

Sit with it.

Feel into it.

Let harmony carry you forward.

love & harmony

october 13

"The shoe that fits one person pinches another; there is no recipe for living that suits all cases."
-Carl Jung

We are all different.

What works perfectly for one person, might fail for another.

What is the worst idea ever for one person, might be the golden ticket for another.

Be mindful of this when being given advice.

Be mindful of this when giving advice.

love & living

october 14

"Listen. I wish I could tell you it gets
better. But, it doesn't get better.
You get better."
–Joan Rivers

Life will throw bizarre things at you over and
over again.

Joys, sorrows, confusions, blisses.

This is the stuff of life.

The brilliance of life is you will learn how to
experience all of it.

You will build a greater capacity to be with all
the things.

It is worth it.

love & learning

october 15

"We were all born with a certain degree of power. The key to success is discovering this innate power and using it daily to deal with whatever challenges come our way."
-Les Brown

What is your innate power?

Today, choose one part of your being that fuels you.

Lead with this power today.

You will be able to face any challenges that the day brings.

love & power

october 16

"Art and love are the same thing:
It's the process of seeing yourself in
things that are not you."
-Chuck Klosterman

Today, as an experiment, look for yourself outside of yourself.

Look for yourself in things that are not you.

You will find you in Art, which is an Art.

You will find you in Love, which takes Love.

love & art

october 17

"The truly free man is the one who can turn down an invitation to dinner without giving an excuse."
–Jules Renard

It's totally okay to say no without a reason.

Give it a go, today.

Say no without a reason, excuse, or explanation.

Perhaps it sounds as simple as:

"I won't be doing that."

"No, thank you."

"Not, today, buttercup."

love & freedom

october 18

"You'll have to forgive me, it's not me, it's my mind."
-Columbo

You and your mind are not the same.

You and your thoughts are not the same.

You get to call the shots.

It just may take a little practice.

love & wisdom

october 19

"It's a terrible thing in life to wait until you're ready."
-Denise Duffield-Thomas

No need to wait.

Jump in before you are ready.

Because (shhh...secret) no one is ever really ready.

love & leaping

october 20

"Imagination is more important than knowledge. Knowledge is limited. Imagination encircles the world."
–Albert Einstein

Today, make space to IMAGINE.

Let go of the reasons things can't be...

Let go of the reasons they are hard...

Let go of what you know...

Let go of the way things have to be...

Let go of your limits...

Give your brain the gift of imagining all that could be.

love & creation

october 21

"The world needs dreamers and the world needs doers. But above all, the world needs dreamers who do."
-Sarah Ban Breathnach

Take time to dream.

Take time to do something that will bring that dream to life.

love & dreaming

october 22

*"The only way to have a friend
is to be one."*
-Ralph Waldo Emerson

Be a friend today.

Reach out to a friend you've had for years.

Make plans with people you enjoy being with.

Share a smile or laugh with someone new.

Friendships don't happen by accident.

Friendships are created.

You can be the creator.

love & friendship

october 23

"If you do not change direction, you may end up where you are heading."
-Lao Tzu

If you don't like where you're going, you best be changing direction!

If you like where you're going, hurray! Onward!

If you don't know where you are headed, look up. Do you like what you see?

love & changes

october 24

"Even the rich are hungry for love, for being cared for, for being wanted, for having someone to call their own."
-Mother Theresa

As humans, we all desire the same things.

We all want love.

We all want to be cared for.

We all want to be wanted.

We all want to have someone to call our own.

Beyond our possessions, our armor, and our accoutrements, we are remarkably similar.

Look for the similarities.

love & humanity

october 25

"There is no remedy for love
but to love more."
-Henry David Thoreau

Love is action, thought, dreams and decisions.

Love is hope, creation, smiles, and vision.

Love is curiosity, remembrance, wonder, and leaning back.

Love is separation, freedom, courage, and laughter.

Love is speaking, silence, comfort, and kindness.

When love feels too much, love more.

love & more of it

october 26

"Lord, make me an instrument of thy peace. Where there is hatred, let me sow love."
-St. Francis of Assisi

Today, sow a little love.

Today, sow a little peace.

You needn't know how or where.

Ask for guidance.

Let peace and love flow through you.

love & peace

october 27

"We need the compassion and the courage to change the conditions that support our suffering. Those conditions are things like ignorance, bitterness, negligence, clinging, and holding on."
-Sharon Salzberg

Are you willing to let go of these conditions?

Are you willing to let go of your suffering?

It seems odd that we would hold onto things that cause us suffering. And yet, many of us do.

Reflect today. What is causing you suffering that you could let go of? Do you have the courage to do so?

love & courage

october 28

"*Imagine all the people living life in peace. You may say I'm a dreamer, but I'm not the only one. I hope someday you'll join us, and the world will be as one.*"
-John Lennon

Let us all keep dreaming.

Let us all keep living life in peace, as best we can.

love & unity

october 29

"Talk to yourself like you would to someone you love."
-Brené Brown

The words we use with ourselves matter.

Both in how we speak to others about ourselves - and how we think of ourselves in our own heads.

Today, practice speaking the kindest words to yourself.

Your soul will thank you.

love & language

october 30

"Love is union with somebody, or something, outside oneself, under the condition of retaining the separateness and integrity of one's own self."
-Erich Fromm

Real love does not include losing yourself.

To have love, we find union with it,
but retain our own separateness and integrity.

No worries, you get to keep being you.

love & union

october 31

"I learned that courage was not the absence of fear, but the triumph over it. The brave man is not he who does not feel afraid, but he who conquers that fear."
–Nelson Mandela

Whether you are afraid or not, when things are worth doing, you can find a way.

Not letting the fear stop you is courage.

love & courage

november

november 1

"Love yourself first, and everything else falls in line. You really have to love yourself to get anything done in this world."
–Lucille Ball

Show yourself some love today.

Feel this love in your heart.

This may take some time, but it's worth it.

Everything will fall into place.

love & order

november 2

"The way to change the world is through individual responsibility and taking local action in your own community."
-Jeff Bridges

What local action can you take to change the world?

Wink, wink, nudge, nudge,
it rhymes with GOAT.

love & freedom

november 3

"If we couldn't laugh we would all go insane."
-Robert Frost

Once, I was out on a lake in an absolute stunner of a boat with many members of my family. The motor stopped working, it was dark out, anyone who knew anything about boats had been imbibing and the sounds the motor were making were pretty scary. In that moment, adrift in the dark, my mother, my brother and I were convinced that the boat would explode and we were facing our imminent death. We laughed and laughed.

We probably looked cuckoo, but we got back to shore safe and smiling. Thanks to the woman that - no joke - jumped in the water and pulled us to shore by a rope.

Since then, I've laughed through some very rough and painful times. I don't care if I looked crazy. Laughter got me through.

Laughter can get us through.

love & laughter

november 4

"There is no greater power in Heaven or on Earth than pure, unconditional love. The nature of the God force, the unseen intelligence in all things, which causes the material world and is the center of both the spiritual and physical plane, is best described as pure, unconditional love."
-Wayne Dyer

How brilliant it is to feel pure, unconditional love.

The sun shining on us. The water flowing to us. Planting seeds and having them grow. The consistency of sunrise and sunset and the tides.

These are all pure, unconditional love.

love & the sun

november 5

"Gratitude is riches.
Complaint is poverty."
 -Doris Day

Just for today, set the poor words
of complaint aside, and replace these with rich
words of gratitude.

love & riches

november 6

"As a single footstep will not make a path on the earth, so a single thought will not make a pathway in the mind. To make a deep physical path, we walk again and again. To make a deep mental path, we must think over and over the kind of thoughts we wish to dominate our lives."
-Henry David Thoreau

If we feel plagued by negative thoughts, guilt, worries, it can feel very frustrating to have them continue to dance around our heads. When a new meditation or mantra doesn't wipe them out instantly, it's frustrating.

Your mind is no different from a path in the woods.

Walk the path daily, on the earth or in your mind. Be selective which paths you take.

Celebrate each healthy, loving path you take and know in time these paths become the open, clear ones.

love & consistency

november 7

"Do not let the behavior of others destroy your inner peace."
−The 14th Dalai Lama Tenzin Gyatso

We can not change the behavior of others.

We can change how we respond to it.

Today, let us focus on our responses.

Breathe in peace.

Breathe out peace.

Be gentle with that kind heart of yours as you learn.

Be gentle.

Go easy.

love & gentleness

november 8

"It isn't what you have or who you are or where you are or what you are doing that makes you happy or unhappy. It is what you think about it."
-Dale Carnegie

'If I could only find the right guy, I'd be happy.'
'If I could just quit this job, I'd be happy.'
'Well, if I could only win the lottery.'
'What I really need right now is a hug, a cup of coffee, and a million dollars.'

YES, AND - all these thoughts push happiness to some future, imaginary time.

The thing about our amazing human brain and body is that we have the power to stop and be happy regardless of circumstance.

For those that think it's hogwash, it will be.

For those who think it's right, it will be.

Guess who's happier?

love & happiness

november 9

"Gratitude can transform common days into thanksgivings, turn routine jobs into joy, and change ordinary opportunities into blessings."
–William Arthur Ward

Today, practice gratitude for all things.

Gratitude for the routine.

Gratitude for the ordinary.

Gratitude for the common.

Watch things change.

love & gratitude

november 10

"To oppose something is to maintain it."
-Ursula K. LeGuin

What are you fighting against?

What are you resisting?

What are you complaining about?

Fighting against something, ironically,
builds it up. It gives it power.

Today, rather than fighting against, pick
something to fight for.

Pick something to build.

Focus your energy and your thoughts on that.

That which we were fighting will, in time,
fall away.

love & releasing

november 11

"'Thank you' is the best prayer that anyone could say. I say that one a lot. Thank you expresses extreme gratitude, humility, understanding."
-Alice Walker

Let our gratitude for each moment, each blessing, each kindred spirit, each heart beating, each smile we come across, be our prayer.

love & gratitude

november 12

"The greatest healing therapy is friendship and love."
-Hubert H. Humphrey

Look at the week ahead.

Where can you add more friendship?

Where can you add more love?

We can all use some of that therapy.

love & healing

november 13

"Invent your world. Surround yourself with people, color, sounds, and work that nourish you."
-Susan Ariel Rainbow Kennedy

Nourishment is more than the food we eat.

It is how we feed all our senses - what see, hear, taste, touch, smell.

It is who we are with and what work we do - what we read and what we watch.

All of this can nourish us, poison us, or be empty filler.

What will we choose?

love & nourishment

november 14

"There's only one corner of the universe
you can be certain of improving,
and that's your own self."
–Aldous Huxley

Some days the home improvements our
universe needs feel wildly overwhelming.

Breathe deep.

Trust that caring for and loving yourself is a
most important corner of the universe to
focus on.

Greening your heart will, in fact, green your
world.

love & certainty

november 15

"You cannot protect yourself from sadness without protecting yourself from happiness."
-Jonathan Safran Foer

It can be very tempting to numb out and freeze our hearts to protect ourselves from being hurt.

Sad thing is this keeps us from happiness as well.

So when you are feeling sad, welcome it.

For if you can feel the sadness, that means you'll be able to feel the happiness.

Allow all of it.

love & happiness

november 16

"Gratitude is the healthiest of all human emotions. The more you express gratitude for what you have the more likely you will have even more to be grateful for."
–Zig Ziglar

If we focus on what we are lacking and what we need, it lands us in a place of suffering.

If we focus on what we have now, and let gratitude spread throughout our head, heart, and body, a wild thing happens...

Even more shows up for us to be grateful for.

What are three things you are grateful for right now?

love & gratitude

november 17

"I've got nothing to do today but smile."
-Simon and Garfunkel

Your assignment for the day: SMILE.

That's it.

Focus on smiling.

Your heart, body and mind will thank you.

love & smiles

november 18

"The essence of life does not consist in the lushness of your possessions, but in the richness of your heart."
-Roy T. Bennett

You have more than enough.

You are more than enough.

Cultivate the riches of your heart.

Giving and receiving warmth, joy, and love.

love & riches

november 19

"Too many of us are not living our dreams because we are living our fears."
–Les Brown

"I can't."

So many times, it's not that we can't, it's that we won't, because we are afraid.

What are your fears keeping you from today?

Live your dream.

love & dreaming

november 20

"It's very important that we re-learn the art of resting and relaxing. Not only does it help prevent the onset of many illnesses that develop through chronic tension and worrying; it allows us to clear our minds, focus, and find creative solutions to problems."
-Thich Nhat Hanh

In our busy-busy, work-work-work world, so many people are very good at what they do, diligent and productive at their work, but reap little of the joy or satisfaction from it. They don't know how to rest, relax, and receive.

Rest is considered a treat you receive when work is done.

But since work is never done in this society we currently find ourselves in - there is always more to do - rest is elusive.

What if we introduced 3 minutes to just breathe? Or stretch our legs and walk? Or gaze out windows?

love & rest

november 21

"*One thing: you have to walk, and create the way by your walking; you will not find a ready-made path. It is not so cheap, to reach to the ultimate realization of truth. You will have to create the path by walking yourself; the path is not ready-made, lying there and waiting for you. It is just like the sky: the birds fly, but they don't leave any footprints. You cannot follow them; there are no footprints left behind.*"
-Osho

If you are working through family drama, if you are creating a business, if you are an artist, if you are in a relationship, if you are letting go of habits or addictions, if you are shaking off negative thoughts, and it all feels so hard...

Take comfort. You are walking a path that is not ready-made. You are creating a new path, with a higher purpose. Keep going.

love & trailblazing

november 22

"If you cannot get rid of the family skeleton, you may as well make it dance."
-George Bernard Shaw

If we are truthful, all of our family stories are complex.

We may be walking into rooms with a wild mix of emotions, loss, pleasure, gratitude, fear, joy.

Let the whirlwind be.

All families have skeletons.

And remember: it is not your job to stop them or to hide them. When you try to stop them or to hide them, the skeletons still win.

Let the skeletons dance.

Let them do their thing.

You be you.

love & dancing

november 23

"The folly of endless consumerism sends us on a wild goose-chase for happiness through materialism."
-Bryant H. McGill

You have everything you need to be happy and joyful.

Today, whatever you are doing, consider, will this action bring me happiness? Or is it a wild goose chase?

Where and how can I share love, meaning, connection, happiness, joyfulness, gratitude, and overflowing abundance today?

love & happiness

november 24

"In the day-to-day, farm work is stress relief for me. At the end of the day, I love having this other career - my anti-job - that keeps me in shape and gives me control over a vegetal domain."
-Barbara Kingsolver

What's your anti-job?

If you don't have one, what WOULD it be?

Make some time for it today.

(((And, yes, daydreaming about it counts.)))

love & relief

november 25

"I celebrate both my uniqueness and my connection with all that is."
–Jonathan Lockwood Hule

What is your blessed uniqueness is also a reflection, a connection with, the grand beauty of universal energy.

By cherishing and expressing your uniqueness you give voice, body and action to all that is, to God, to spirit, to this divine mystery.

Be that. The world needs you as you.

Don't be stingy. Sharing is caring.

love & celebration

november 26

"At the center of your being you have the answer, you know who you are and you know what you want."
-Lao Tzu

Who are you?

What do you want in life?

You were born for more than waking, working, zoning out in front of screens (even very entertaining screens), sleeping, on repeat.

You may be living an exquisitely meaningful, fulfilling life. YES!!!

Or you may ache for something different. Something feels missing. What were you born for?

At the center of your being. You know.

There just may be some "shoulds", "shouldn'ts", "can'ts" and fears in the way.

love & being

november 27

"In every community, there is work to be done. In every nation, there are wounds to heal. In every heart, there is the power to do it."
-Marianne Williamson

It's easier to point fingers or throw hands up, sometimes, when it comes to healing the world - or ourselves.

Whether we are looking at humans or whole worlds, healing is not easy, but it is natural.

Today, make some time to intentionally heal.

Give yourself - and the world - this gift.

love & healing

november 28

*"Let food be thy medicine
and medicine be thy food."*
-Hippocrates

Yum, yum.

Feed your body well today.

Your body will thank you.

love & nourishment

november 29

"Life is a balance of holding on and letting go."
-Rumi

Is there anything you're holding onto that it is time to let go of?

Sometimes, we hold on without even realizing it.

Holding on can be a habit, our routine, in our comfort zone.

If you choose to hold on, do it on purpose.

And if you choose to let go, let that be on purpose too.

love & balance

november 30

"Always forgive your enemies.
Nothing annoys them so much."
-Oscar Wilde

Forgiveness is actually quite self-serving.

Be self-serving.

Forgive for YOU.

Everyone wins.

Even the annoyed ones.

love & forgiveness

december

december 1

"Folks are usually about as happy as they make their minds up to be."
-Abraham Lincoln

How happy will you make your mind up to be today?

love & happiness

december 2

"This is my simple religion. There is no need for temples; no need for complicated philosophy. Our own brain, our own heart is our temple; the philosophy is kindness."
-The 14th Dalai Lama Tenzin Gyatso

We love making things complicated, don't we?

Today, keep it simple.

Just be kind.

No reasons, theories, excuses, judgments or complicated philosophies needed.

love & kindness

december 3

"What we do for ourselves dies with us, what we do for others and the world remains and is immortal."
-Albert Pine

Today, do something that will be immortal.

A word of encouragement, a gift, a hand up, a seed planted- all these live on outside of you.

love & immortality

december 4

"Life is a mirror and will reflect back to the thinker what he thinks into it."
-Ernest Holmes

Hey you, with that big, beautiful
brain of yours.

What will you think into the world?

love & thoughts

december 5

"You may not always have a comfortable life and you will not always be able to solve all of the world's problems at once but don't ever underestimate the importance you can have because history has shown us that courage can be contagious and hope can take on a life of its own."
-Michelle Obama

You don't need to solve all the world's problems today.

Show courage.

Have hope.

It's contagious.

And that's just the sort of thing the world needs most.

love & courage

december 6

"Happiness is when what you think, what you say, and what you do are in harmony."
-Mahatma Gandhi

Thoughts.

Words.

Actions.

In the wild kaleidoscope of our lives,
let us bring these ever closer in harmony.

love & harmony

december 7

"If more of us valued food and cheer and song above hoarded gold, it would be a merrier world."
-J.R.R. Tolkien

Today, celebrate food.

Celebrate cheer.

Celebrate song.

For each of their own individual beauty.

We are so very rich.

love & merriment

december 8

"True enjoyment comes from activity of the mind and exercise of the body; the two are ever united."
-Wilhelm von Humboldt

Today, do at least one thing to exercise the body and at least one thing to exercise the mind.

Both will be doubly happy.

love & unity

december 9

"I celebrate both my uniqueness and my connection with all that is."
−Jonathan Lockwood Huie

You are you.

You are we.

We are all connected.

We breathe each other's air and drink each other's water.

love & connection

december 10

"If only you could sense how important you are to the lives of those you meet; how important you can be to people you may never even dream of. There is something of yourself that you leave at every meeting with another person."
-Fred Rogers

You matter.

More than you'll ever know.

Today, open your eyes, slow down and leave something special with each person you meet.

love & connection

december 11

"*I have just three things to teach:
simplicity, patience, compassion. These
three are your greatest treasures.*"
-Lao Tzu

Our greatest treasures are not things that we
acquire.

It's what we have in our hearts, already,
underneath.

Simplicity.

Patience.

Compassion.

All are with you now.

love & treasures

december 12

"Conflict cannot survive without your participation."
-Wayne Dyer

'Tis the season for LOVE - with sides of drama, debates, and elephants in rooms.

Hurray!

Conflicts arise.

This is the nature of living.

But a conflict won't survive without the flame being tended to.

You can choose to walk away.

You can choose what conversations you'll participate in.

love & elephants

december 13

"The forgiving state of mind is a magnetic power for attracting good. No good thing can be withheld from the forgiving state of mind."
-Catherine Ponder

Forgive here, forgive there,
forgive everywhere!

Forgive others.

Forgive ourselves.

For example, what would it feel like to have the "shoulds" and "shouldn't haves" released from our minds?

Forgiveness gives us power to release these judgments, and other gobbly-gook that gets in the way of receiving. In this way, forgiveness opens us up for good we couldn't have even imagined.

love & forgiveness

december 14

"It is good to have an end to journey towards, but it is the journey that matters in the end."
-Ursula Le Guin

If you are working towards your end goal and miserable each moment, I have a surprise for you.

Chances are you won't enjoy the end goal either.

Stop what you are doing.

Look around.

This is what life is all about.

This moment.

Set your goals. Work towards them.

And make space to love this very moment, too.

It is filled with love and goodness.

love & every moment

december 15

"A wise man once said nothing."
-Anonymous

.
.
.

love & wisdom

december 16

"A goal without a plan is just a wish."
-Antoine de Saint-Exupéry

What goals do you have for the year ahead?

How serious are you about them?

Are they goals that you are really treating as wishes?

Is this the year to finally eat healthy/meditate /eliminate debt/take that trip/find true love/get a hot tub/having a rocking business/make millions/write a book?

Whatever your goals, get planning!

Make those beautiful dream-wishes of yours reality.

love & creation

december 17

"You get what you really want, not what you ask for."
–Barbara Stanny

Oooh, sit still and ask.

What do you *really* want?

Not what you *think* you want.

What does your heart yearn for?

It's a mysterious thing, but sometimes the heart is yearning for comfort, the known, simplicity. Sometimes we yearn for chaos or contention, simply because that is what is more familiar.

If what you are asking for - and what your soul aches for - are not aligned - chances are it won't be showing up for you.

love & alignment

december 18

"Love is the capacity to take care, to protect, to nourish."
-Thich Nhat Hanh

How can you take exquisite care of yourself?

How can you protect yourself today?

How will you nourish yourself today?

Will you care for yourself as you care for others?

Your body and soul will be so very grateful.

love & nourishment

december 19

"The morning breeze has secrets to tell you. Do not go back to sleep."
-Rumi

Are you awake?

Are you sleep-walking?

Wake, listen...

What secrets await you?

You won't know if you fill the silence.

Wake, listen...

What wisdom awaits you?

You won't know if you numb it out.

Wake, listen...

The morning breeze has a gift for you.

What will it be?

love & wisdom

december 20

"All the suffering, stress, and addiction come from not realizing you already are what you are looking for."
-Jon Kabat-Zinn

There is no need to do - be - accumulate - coerce - manifest - struggle - more.

Be open to all you have and what you are, in all your beauty, in your abundance.

You have enough.

You are enough.

love & gratitude

december 21

"I will love the light for it shows me the way, yet I will endure the darkness because it shows me the stars."
–Og Mandino

On the Winter Solstice, we celebrate the longest night of the year.

We celebrate its beauty.

The beauty of the darkness.

For the brilliance it opens up for us.

We can have so much love for all of it.

love & darkness

december 22

"Stillness and empty space give rise to painful feelings. Rather than experience the pain, busyness becomes your drug of choice."
-Barbara Stanny

"How are you?"

"So busy."

How do you react to a moment alone in quiet?

Busyness numbs just as drugs, alcohol, or TV.

It is one of the few drugs that may make you look good.

Notice if your busyness has become an escape.

Cultivate stillness. Cultivate quiet.

Magic arises when we learn to be with it all.

love & stillness

december 23

"The arts, quite simply, nourish the soul. They sustain, comfort, inspire. There is nothing like that exquisite moment when you first discover the beauty of connecting with others in celebration of larger ideals and shared wisdom."
-Gordon Gee

If you feel separate, down-hearted or disconnected, seek out art.

It is all around.

Be with it.

Create it.

Let it surround you.

Let it nourish you.

love & art

december 24

"Try not to resist the changes that come your way. Instead let life live through you."
-Rumi

Change is inevitable.

And yet, so often, we rebel against it, mourn it, dread it, do a million little - or big - things to ward it off.

Learning to accept change, letting "life live through you", is an entirely different way of living.

love & freedom

december 25

"This is a wonderful day. I've never seen this one before."
–Maya Angelou

May we enjoy each holiday - and every day - as a holy day - new and fresh and never seen before.

May we celebrate the old, create the new, and love more love than we've ever experienced before.

love & wonder

december 26

"To love oneself is the beginning of a life-long romance."
-Oscar Wilde

Swoon.

Let's get some head-over-heels, smoochy smoochy, big, huge love going for you.

You deserve it.

How can you show yourself some big love today?

love & kindness

december 27

"The more you praise and celebrate your life, the more there is in life to celebrate."
-Oprah Winfrey

Today it's my birthday!!! I have been so crazy blessed to have these years on this earth.

How many do you have?

Yay! Celebrate each one!

So much to love. You are a TRIUMPH!

love & celebration

december 28

"If you begin to understand what you are without trying to change it, then what you are undergoes a transformation."
-Jiddu Krishnamurti

Whoa.

There's a puzzler for you.

Just as all of life.

If we stop to look.

What are you?

What are you if there's nothing to change?

love & wonder

december 29

"And if tonight my soul may find her peace in sleep, and sink in good oblivion, and in the morning wake like a new-opened flower then I have been dipped again in God, and new-created."
-D. H. Lawrence

Get a little extra rest today, dear one.

Sleeping, dreaming, nurturing, nourishing.

You will rest with spirit and arise anew.

love & connection

december 30

"You have to enjoy life. Always be surrounded by people that you like, people who have a nice conversation. There are so many positive things to think about."
-Sophia Loren

You get to choose...

What you focus on.

Who you talk to.

The conversations you want to be in.

This does not mean running to the hills and avoiding responsibilities.

But we can be in conversations we need to be in differently.

And we can choose to surround ourselves with more and more of what lights up our soul with joy.

love & joy

december 31

"For last year's words belong to last year's language and next year's words await another voice. And to make an end is to make a beginning."
-T. S. Eliot

Whether you are focused on giving the past year a good ol' shove...

Or giving the new year a great big hug...

Or maybe a little bit o' both...

The parts we'd like to shove and leave behind, can be our greatest teachers. They may bring us through doors we never would have opened otherwise.

Let us honor and be grateful for all of it.

Let us walk into the year ahead with eyes wide open, awake, in love with our lives and those we share it with. Blessings. And so very much to celebrate.

love & celebration

21-Day Manifesting Experience

With Elizabeth B. Hill

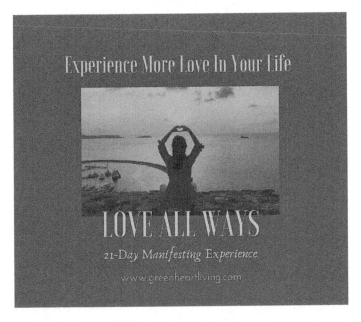

Join Elizabeth as she guides you through 21 days of 20-minute manifesting meditations designed to enhance the experience of love in your life.

Each Manifesting Meditation Includes:
Centering, Words of Wisdom, Pranayama (Breathing Practices to Balance the Nervous System), and a Guided Mantra Meditation.

Access here:
www.greenheartliving.com/love-all-ways

ALSO BY ELIZABETH B. HILL

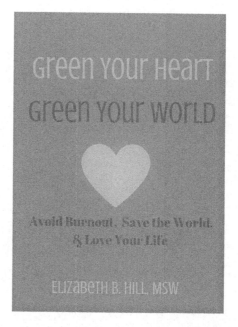

"Green Your Heart, Green Your World" is a gift for the helpers: nonprofit professionals, teacher, parents, nurses, social workers, caregivers, community leaders, volunteers and anyone who spends their days in service to others. This book contains a wealth of soulful practices to help people avoid burnout, save the world and love their lives. Readers can expect to be inspired to share their own unique light with the world while being empowered to stay healthy, happy and whole in the process.

Obtain your copy on Amazon or at
www.greenheartliving.com

Select Bibliography

Bernstein, Gabrielle. *The Universe Has Your Back: Transform Fear to Faith*. Hay House, 2016.

Casey, Karen. *Each Day a New Beginning*. Hazelden, 1991.

Chopra, Deepak. *The Seven Spiritual Laws of Success – A Practical Guide to the Fulfillment of Your Dreams*. New World Library: 1994.

Gibran, Kahlil. *The Prophet*. 1923. Rpt. Alfred A. Knopf, 2000.

Gilbert, Elizabeth. *Big Magic*. River Head Books, 2015.

Nhat Hanh, Thich. *Peace is Every Step: The Path of Mindfulness in Everyday Life*. Bantam Book, 1991.

Rosenfeld, Laura and Dr. Melva Green. *Breathing Room: Open Your Heart by Decluttering Your Home*. Atria Books/Beyond Words, 2014.

Stanny, Barbara. *Overcoming Underearning: A Five-Step Plan to a Richer Life by Barbara Stanny*. Collins Publishers, 2005.

Stanny, Barbara. *Sacred Success: A Course in Financial Miracles*. BenBella Books, 2014.

Williamson, Marianne. *A Return to Love: Reflections on the Principles of A Course in Miracles*. HarperOne, 1992.

Select Internet Sources

www.brainyquote.com

www.goodreads.com

www.habitsforwellbeing.com

Follow Elizabeth

greenheartliving.com

facebook.com/greenheartliving

facebook.com/groups/21daymanifestingexperience

instagram.com/greenheartlovenotes

Would You Like Elizabeth to Speak to Your Group?

email liz@greenheartliving.com

Interested in Mentoring with Elizabeth or a Green Heart Living Coach?

email liz@greenheartliving.com

About The Author

Elizabeth B. Hill, MSW is the author of "Green Your Heart, Green Your World: Avoid Burnout, Save the World and Love Your Life" and the founder of Green Heart Living, which provides coaching, education, healing modalities, and resources to help make the world a more loving and peaceful place - one person at a time.

Elizabeth has special expertise in helping those with anxiety and high-stress lives to cope and get the results they desire in their professional life, wellness, and relationships. Trained as a social worker, yoga teacher, and life coach, she weaves creativity, spirituality, and mindfulness into her work with clients.

Elizabeth lives in Connecticut with her family and the neighborhood bears. Learn more about her and her work at www.greenheartliving.com

Made in the USA
Columbia, SC
01 March 2020

88505617R00222